PRAISE FOR
Everyday Business Storytelling

"It's rare to find a partner that can directly impact the performance of your sales leaders. Janine and Lee have been instrumental in helping us achieve success since 2014, empowering our sales leaders to tell better stories."

—**LAURA MORAROS,** *Head, Global Marketing Solutions Learning and Enablement,* ***Facebook***

"It has always been challenging to find a comprehensive development solution that helps teach employees how to create and share compelling, audience-centric business stories. This approach is grounded in real scenarios and case studies that anyone can relate to. If you're looking to up-level your skillset in storytelling and drive business conversations forward, get this book!"

—**STACY SALVALAGGIO,** *Vice President, Retail Operations,* ***Aritzia*** *and former Global Senior Director, Learning and Development,* ***McDonald's***

"There's no greater skill and ingenuity to propel your career than the ability to translate data insights into clear, authentic narratives. This book is the winning formula for any executive."

—**SYDNEY SAVION,** *Chief Learning Officer,* ***Air New Zealand***

"Lee and Janine have shown you can transform technical information and make it digestible in everyday communications. A must-read. Bravo."

—**AYELET STEINITZ,** *Head, Global Strategic Alliances,* ***Microsoft***

"If you've caught on to the value of business storytelling, this book is absolutely vital. Not only does it provide a straightforward structure for building business stories, but it lays out how to 'flex' your narrative based on real-life situations. One of the best productivity books I've ever read!"

—**JOSH COY,** *Director, Hotel Openings - Training Delivery,* ***Marriott International***

"Storytelling is a critical component of being an inspirational leader within our organization. By using this framework and integrating it into our top talent and leadership programs, we have begun to reset the way we approach conversations, meetings and presentations. Having worked with Lee and Janine at two Fortune 500 companies, this book reveals their talent for teaching people to quickly decode complex information in a very practical and applicable way."

—**SHARON BRITTON,** *Director, Global Talent and*
Leadership Development, **Medtronic**

"It's not often you find a no-nonsense approach and repeatable methodology that can directly impact your business and talent pool. We started adopting these storytelling principles back in 2015 and have never looked back. This is the ESSENTIAL guide!"

—**JANE HOSKISSON,** *Director, Learning and Development,*
International Air Transport Association

"In their book *Everyday Business Storytelling,* Lee and Janine walk their talk. Having experienced their incredible instructor-led class on this topic, I was thrilled to see that their book is every bit as lively, visually educational and boiled down to the good stuff... Just like your presentations will be when you follow their advice."

—**SUZ HAHN,** *Manager, Learning and Development,* **Daimler**

"The difference between storytelling in Hollywood and in business isn't as stark as you think. In writing, plot pulls characters through conflict, but story is why we care. In business, if a company tells a story that customers care about, its product becomes more relevant and desirable. Every company wants the same Hollywood ending: become a success story. This book can help write that script for any business."

—**RON RAPPAPORT,** *Writer and Producer,* **Netflix**

"The world is flooded with data but lacking in a simple, logical way to use it for better decision-making. Storytelling is without a doubt, the way to go. This approach captured in this tell-all book has been a gamechanger for our team. An investment worth every penny!"

—**BRIAN LAAKSO,** *Senior Supply Chain Process Analyst,* ***Columbia Sportsware***

"We were all born storytellers and when we do it well we inspire and connect with the people we care about. I've watched Janine and Lee strengthen this skill within hundreds of people in our work together at Apple and Facebook and I'm thrilled they're sharing their unique approach in a book that will quickly become a go-to-resource for leaders at all levels."

—**TOM FLOYD,** *Former Head of Manager Effectiveness,* ***Facebook,*** *and Founder,* ***Flouracity***

"Our team was always great at getting the information out of their heads, not so great at making their audience care about it. We've worked with Lee and Janine for over a decade to turn this around. I'm thrilled to get my hands on a book that's based on their indispensable storytelling techniques."

—**MEGAN GAILEY,** *Managing Director, Corporate Services,* ***Maxim Integrated***

"Janine and Lee underscore the need to build a culture of storytelling. They provide their recipe on building a powerful, authentic narrative— including the ingredients, science, and adaptations to reach every audience and spur action."

—**CATHERINE LACOUR,** *Chief Marketing Officer,* ***Blackbaud***

"We're often told that we need to turn our numbers into narratives... this book does just that! Thank you for sharing this practical storytelling approach that, until now, has only been shared with your Fortune 500 clients."

—**LAUREN GOLDSTEIN,** *Principal and Chief Revenue Officer,* ***ANNUITAS*** *and Co-Founder and Board Member,* ***Women in Revenue***

JANINE KURNOFF | LEE LAZARUS

everyday
BUSINESS
STORYTELLING

CREATE, SIMPLIFY, AND ADAPT

A VISUAL NARRATIVE

FOR ANY AUDIENCE

WILEY

Published by John Wiley & Sons, Inc., Hoboken, New Jersey.
Published simultaneously in Canada.

'TPC,' the TPC logo, 'THE PRESENTATION COMPANY,' the THE PRESENTATION COMPANY logo, 'FRANKENDECK',
'THE FOUR SIGNPOSTS', and 'THE PIVOT' are trademarks of The Presentation Company, LLC.

For general information on our other products and services or for technical support, please contact our
Customer Care Department within the United States at (800) 762-2974, outside the United States at (317)
572-3993 or fax (317) 572-4002.

Wiley publishes in a variety of print and electronic formats and by print-on-demand. Some material included
with standard print versions of this book may not be included in e-books or in print-on-demand. If this book
refers to media such as a CD or DVD that is not included in the version you purchased, you may download this
material at http://booksupport.wiley.com. For more information about Wiley products, visit www.wiley.com.

Library of Congress Cataloging-in-Publication Data is Available:
ISBN 978-1-119-70466-9 (Paperback)
ISBN 978-1-119-70469-0 (ePDF)
ISBN 978-1-119-80967-8 (ePub)

COVER DESIGN: PAUL MCCARTHY
AUTHORS' PHOTO: KITTA BODMER PHOTOGRAPHY

SKY10035459_072522

Contents

Storytelling Is How We Move Business Forward

YOU LOVE STORIES. WE LOVE STORIES.

Everybody loves a good story (because we're *human*). But many of us find it really hard to invite storytelling into our everyday business lives. Why? Because we're not Hollywood screenwriters or advertising gurus (at least most of us aren't). We're business people who must present both internally and externally, up, across and down the organization. And most of the time we have to present fairly *unsexy* content. You know, the quarterly business review, a product update, a change management initiative, and so on. To the majority of us, it's not obvious how to authentically incorporate storytelling into our daily work lives.

Instead, we resort to what we *do* know. We leverage existing content for a "quick fix." We grab our latest slide deck that we (or our co-worker) built as a starting point, and from there we cobble together slides. We load up on bulleted text. We pile in every chart we can find. We even add in some "pretty" slides that we found on the corporate portal from the marketing team. We have a very technical term for this type of incoherent, hodgepodge communication. We call it a ***Frankendeck*™**.

You've seen them. *Frankendecks* show up in our meetings and flood our inbox. And the results can be scary! Your audience is left confused. There's no clear message or call to action. And ultimately, you've missed an opportunity to influence a decision and drive business forward.

Can we all agree, no more *Frankendecks*?

What if there was a simple, repeatable, practical, storytelling approach that could help you (and your team) craft a narrative with a visual strategy to support it? What if you had an easy-to-follow framework that let you kick-start your story. Every. Single. Time. This is what we have been building for two decades: storytelling that is second nature for business communication both verbally and visually. No scrambling. No "quick fix" results. No *Frankendecks*.

FRANKENDECKS ARE THE PLACE WHERE GOOD IDEAS ARE LOST AND DECISIONS ARE STALLED.

We fully (yes, fully) understand the resistance

We hear you. You're busy. You have no time. You present to complicated audiences with diverse needs. Your boss doesn't have patience for a "story" with a big reveal. She just needs you to produce three slides for her to present to her manager. Oh, and you've just been told by the "brand police" within your organization to use specific assets like defined templates and graphics. We get it! *We feel your pain because we, too, have been there.*

And that's precisely why we wrote this book.

Make storytelling relevant and practical to everyone in business—*every day*

We're going to demystify storytelling by arming you with a simple approach that will, once and for all, make storytelling relevant and practical to everyone in business—*every day*. You'll see examples throughout this book, designed to inspire you, that are grounded in scenarios you face every day. Like, how do you flex your narrative when you're told your presentation time has been reduced from 30 minutes to *(gulp)* five minutes? No need to panic. You'll learn a visual storytelling framework that makes it *easy* to adjust things at the last minute.

Story strategy that's great for visual presentations, virtual meetings... or anything else

For the most part, the examples you'll see in this book are very *visual*. Why? Because visuals are a powerful way to humanize your story, build emotion, and compel people to act (see *Chapter 1: Meet the Brain Scientists* to find out why). But it's important to note, to make their impact, visuals *must* support and ultimately enhance your story, not detract from it. This is especially true when you're not always the "storyteller"—the person in the room (or virtual room) to deliver the message.

That said, we'll also show you examples that aren't visual, but still use effective story structure—like when you have to craft an important email or create a one-page overview. In short, we'll show you how to apply fundamental story structure to anything you say, send, deliver, or present. *Anything.*

So what do two sisters from Silicon Valley know about business storytelling?

In 2001, the dot-com-dot-bomb was busting, companies were downsizing, and most of the recent start-ups were getting vaporized. We had both been working in tech for several years and saw it all. Janine was in global sales training at Yahoo! Inc. (and later an on-camera webcast host). Lee was head of marketing communications for two of the fastest-growing Internet and telecommunications market-research firms in the Valley.

We were no strangers to rambling PowerPoint presentations, chockablock with data and no story. We could see how audiences were left perplexed by what they were supposed to know or do. We knew then there had to be a better way to communicate ideas. So we put our minds together and started The Presentation Company (TPC).

Two decades later, our certified women-owned training company has been delivering workshops that help multinational and Fortune 500 companies tell visual stories that powerfully connect with their audience. Along with our amazing, super-human team, we've developed award-winning training and tools that give people the confidence and skills to turn their data and insights into engaging, audience-centric business narratives. We've had the honor of supporting some of the world's largest brands along the way, including Facebook, Nestlé , Hewlett-Packard, Medtronic, Accenture, Marriott, McDonald's, Apple, LEGO, and many more.

And we have observed... a lot

In developing our simple storytelling strategy, we have observed hundreds of organizations with varying paces, workstyles, and cultural norms. We've trained ultra-fast-moving companies. We've trained the slowest dinosaurs. But no matter who we've encountered, we've unmistakably noticed that those with a culture of storytelling are truly winning. They have more cohesive messaging, better team collaboration, and a far better approach to selling their ideas to the world. And there's something else. People who thrive in rich, storytelling ecosystems rapidly rise in their careers.

Storytelling is career gold

In every company we've ever worked with, we've seen how storytelling is an essential ingredient in building mastery of ideas, audience connection, and the power skill everyone wants—executive presence.

Whether you're making a recommendation to your boss's boss, providing a product update, or managing difficult questions from a prospective customer, knowing how to build on a story framework humanizes your content, creates a two-way dialogue, and lets you meet your audience's needs *in the moment.*

Storytelling will help you confidently lead conversations, giving both you and your audience a guideline to where the narrative is going and where it's been. It's *amazing* how much this prevents both confusion and boredom.

We wrote this book because we believe *down to our core* that with some simple guidance and tools, *everyone* can be a great business storyteller. You can be a great business storyteller. Come with us.

Let us show you how.

Janine Lee

PART 1

Once and for all—

Let's Unfluff the Reputation of Business Storytelling

CHAPTER 1

Meet the Brain Scientists

WE ALL AGREE WE LOVE STORIES, RIGHT?

And business storytelling is widely recognized as a great way to sell your ideas. We made this case in the introduction (check it out if you missed it). But many business people don't see "storytelling" as something that is going to be worth their time. It sounds *fluffy* (fluffy is the word we hear most). And so, before we learn how to actually construct a business story, let's—once and for all—*unfluff* the reputation of business storytelling.

Say hello to Roger

Roger Wolcott Sperry discovered something amazing about our brains. He examined a man whose epilepsy was so bad, his corpus callosum (the connector between the right and left hemispheres of the brain) was cut. This was to calm his seizures, and thankfully, it helped. It also let this CalTech psychobiologist observe how each side of the brain functioned independently. Sperry detected that each hemisphere operates with its own perception, concepts, and impulses. The left side is logical, analytic, and verbal. The right side is conceptual, intuitive, and visual. Sperry's split-brain research won the Nobel Prize for Medicine in 1981.[1]

Fascinating. But what's this got to do with storytelling?

Many neuroscientists have continued Sperry's research and observed how it seems that we don't use solely our right brain or our left brain to arrive at a decision, we use both.

WE ARE CONSTANTLY PING-PONGING BACK AND FORTH, BETWEEN OUR LEFT AND RIGHT BRAIN HEMISPHERES.

This process is triggered when we're deciding whether to brew a pot of coffee or splurge at Starbucks. It's triggered when we are craving a venti mocha (450 calories!) but know the Pike Place Roast (5 calories) is healthier. And yes, it is triggered at the office. Should I sign this deal? Should I fund that expansion? Should I hire this candidate?

And, if you're hoping to influence *others* in these decisions, you want to awaken this process.

Storytelling triggers both right- and left-brain thinking

Your left brain is a like a filing cabinet. It looks for patterns and seeks to match new information with existing or known information. So, when *many* facts and data are thrown at it, your left brain tries to process it all, but ultimately, gets overloaded. At that pace, nothing can be categorized, and information doesn't stick. It becomes noise.

Your left brain is like a filing cabinet →

Left Brain

Right Brain

Your right brain lets you feel and imagine things ←

Think back to that meeting (in-person or virtual) where the presenter *flooded* you with all kinds of charts, tables, and bulleted facts. Do you remember any of it? If so, was it the rows of numbers you recall or the *story* that the data told? In all probability, it was the story you remember (if there was one).

We're far more likely to remember stories because they ignite our right brain. Our right brain lets us take in new information and then feel and imagine things. It ignites our creative processing where we leave the realm of the known and begin to envision possible futures— beyond what is already in our mental filing cabinet.

And when you tell stories that are supported by precise data and visuals, it appeals to *both* the creative and logical sides of the brain.

IT'S THE COMBINATION OF STORY, DATA, AND VISUALS THAT WILL SET YOUR IDEAS ON FIRE.

Recently, Stanford Business School professor, Jennifer Aaker performed a test on her own students. One by one, her class presented a pitch. One in ten of them used a story within their pitch. All the others stuck to pure facts and figures. Afterwards, the class was asked to write down what they remembered. It was staggering. A measly 5% of students recalled any statistic, but a whopping 63% could recite one or more of the stories.

Well over ten times the students could remember a story over any single fact.

More brain science proof for storytelling

We know we process the world by batting information between our creative right brains and our logical left brains. But let's meet another brain scientist who found something else very interesting: at the precise point of a decision, we are mainly driven by emotions. *(Humans... we're so dramatic.)*

Meet Antonio

Cognitive neuroscientist **Antonio Damasio** has studied the effects of brain damage on many people. One man he observed, Elliot, had injuries which blunted his emotional processing. What Damasio noticed was fascinating. Elliot *really* struggled to make a decision without emotional stimuli. This discovery became Damasio's famous *Somatic Marker Hypothesis.* He concluded that although we *think* we make decisions based purely on logic, it's *emotions* that actually play a key role at *go time.* As Damasio puts it, "Emotions let us mark things good, bad, or indifferent."

ALTHOUGH WE THINK WE MAKE DECISIONS BASED PURELY ON LOGIC, IT'S EMOTIONS THAT ACTUALLY PLAY A KEY ROLE AT GO TIME.

So we know our brains are divided in two and each side plays a different role to help us process the world. The left side is the filing cabinet of stuff we know. Our right side helps us look beyond the known, tap into our intuition, and imagine possibilities. We also know that—even if we *think* we're purely "Mr. Spock" logical—at the crucial point of decision-making, we are driven by emotions.

Let's meet another brilliant scientist—this time a psychiatrist—to tell us something even more startling about the right brain, the left brain, and the world we live in.

And boy, this really, *really* makes the case for business storytelling...

Greetings, Iain

In his groundbreaking book, *The Master and His Emissary: The Divided Brain and the Making of the Western World,* **Iain McGilchrist** took a hard look at how our right brain and left brain help us see the world. He found that the left brain— dominant in language, speech, and reason— operates in a closed, narrow, and controlled space. Basically, it's our inner bureaucrat. Our right brain, on the other hand, allows us to draw implicit meaning from new information, make inferences, and leap beyond our *known* world. In other words, it's our path to transformation and change.

McGilchrist argues (even laments) that today, we are *over-codifying* our world. The drive to capture and systematize everything (Big Data anyone?) has a very left brain, logical appeal. But, he contends, this obsession with strict measurement stands in the way of the transformational leap driven by our imagination.

This is precisely what is causing one of the major problems in today's workplace.

WE OVER-RELY ON DATA, NUMBERS, STATISTICS, AND ANALYTICS TO COMMUNICATE.

Instead of helping brilliant (or at least *good*) ideas be recognized, data actually gets in the way. We are pointing a firehose of information at decision-makers and saying... *make a decision!*

If you're not yet convinced of the science that shows how injecting emotion sells our ideas and conversely, how data overload stifles our ideas, let's meet one final scientist whose findings point to another way to bring emotion (and attention) to a narrative—visuals.

Well hey, John

Molecular biologist **John Medina**'s book *Brain Rules* says visuals are our most dominant sense and naturally spur our emotions. If they are well-coordinated with your story, they serve as super-efficient Post-it Notes that say: *store this in your memory!* Medina points out that if you "hear a piece of information, three days later you'll remember 10% of it. Add a picture and you'll remember 65% of it." Whoa, that's *six times* more memorable if you display your key ideas visually. Just imagine how much visuals will help when you face that decision-maker on their ninth meeting of the day!

Data and visuals either enrich or confuse your story

When visuals such as charts, infographics, and (simple) text are used to directly support your story, they make your ideas and insights profoundly more memorable. And of course, the science backs this up.

But a caution about visuals. One of the places we struggle most in the business world is overuse of visuals—*especially when it comes to presenting data.* We often pile on the charts and tables to add "weight" to our message in order to really sell it. Unfortunately, this barrage of numbers often has the opposite effect. Keep reading for more about how to get the most out of data (hint: it has everything to do with story).

CHAPTER 2

Data *(Yes, sometimes overused)* Is *Not* the Villain

NOW, DESPITE THE FACT that fire-hosing people with charts can stymie decisions, data is *not* inherently bad. *On the contrary.* Supportive data, used strategically, leads us to great insights about our current situation—as well as opportunities for a brighter future.

If you wrap your data in a story, you'll have a much better chance at making your audience feel something. You'll pique their (right brain) curiosity and their intuition and allow them to take a *mental leap* with you. At the same time, the (left brain) data which *directly supports* your story offers the final justification to get decision-makers to "yes." And it's this left brain/right brain tango that'll give weight to your ideas, further business conversations, and influence decisions.

Data will supercharge your story with insights

To make our business case, we often rely on data, numbers, statistics, and analytics. It is truly the engine of your ideas. But excellent storytellers see value in data not just as a general information dump but for the meaning and insights they bring to a story.

Before you include data, always ask these questions: *Does it support my story? Does it further my narrative? Have I edited it (ferociously) to bring forward great insights?*

DATA WRAPPED IN A **WELL-CRAFTED STORY** IS UNSTOPPABLE

Great data insights show discovery

In his book *Seeing What Others Don't,* Gary Klein offers some clear definitions of insight:

- Insights are *discoveries* based on analysis and interpretation of data.

- Insights change how we understand an issue and *transform our thinking* about ways to create business value.

- Insights shift us toward *a new and better story.*[1]

What stands out about these definitions? For one, the word *discovery*. Discovery implies something new or previously unknown. To find insights in data, look for something completely new like inconsistencies or contradictions, or the opposite—connections and coincidences wherever they are unexpected. Other insights can be found in recurring problems or even a powerful personal anecdote that moved us to adopt a remarkable new point of view.

ANYTHING CAN BE AN INSIGHT AS LONG AS IT HIGHLIGHTS WHAT'S WRONG WITH THE OLD STORY, AND SHOWS HOW MUCH BETTER A NEW ONE COULD BE.

Tame the data dump

But remember, *data on its own are not ideas.* And it can work in both directions. Carefully selected insights can supercharge your proposal, update, or recommendation with power. Offering your audience this education makes you look smart and them *feel* smart (who doesn't love that?). But table after chart after diagram will backfire, causing confusion and resistance.

To build a narrative journey that's going to work, take the time to *discover* the handful of insights that'll move your story forward and make it memorable.

Tame your impulse to show too much raw data.

Data vs. story: A furry experiment

Let's try a super-quick test. Scan the following data about health insurance for pets. First, see the facts and data. Then read the same information wrapped in a story. What version is more memorable and easier to recall?

Go ahead and we'll meet at the other end...

DATA ONLY

Market Stats for Pet Insurance

The global pet insurance market size was valued at USD 5.7 billion in 2018. The global market will reach USD 10.2 billion in 2025. Dog insurance is the largest segment, holding 80.8% of revenue share. Dog accident policies show the steadiest growth at 6.5% over the next five years. Accident and illness insurance coverage dominated the overall industry and accounted for revenue of USD 5.4 billion in 2018. Policies usually cover about 80% of the total veterinary bill.

DATA + STORY

Pet Owners Want to Protect their Pets and their Wallet

Meet 30-year-old Madison. Like so many pet moms and dads, she's crazy about her Labrador, Larry. But with checkups, vaccines, and several altercations at the dog park, Larry was becoming one expensive pup! So Madison looked into pet insurance and much to her surprise, discovered she was not alone. Pet owners spent 5 billion dollars last year on pet insurance worldwide and are projected to spend over 10 billion by 2025. Most insurance is purchased for frisky pups like Larry, for when they get sick or have an accident. But owners like Madison—who can get 80% of Larry's stitches covered—are finding it a huge relief. A giant wag to that!

IN SHORT...

So, what did you think? Will you remember the *data only,* or the *data wrapped in a story?* What helped you glean the most important information about the pet insurance market? Which could you recall if you had to make a decision? The reality is, most of us can take in—and retain—information better when it's presented in the form of a story rather than a pile of data.

A STORY WILL ALWAYS BE MORE MEMORABLE.

So go ahead, free your data from your inner bureaucrat. Combine your facts and data with a succinct story to awaken both the left and right brain. This will ensure your ideas are going to stick with *any* audience.

RECAP

The Neuroscience of Visual Storytelling... *Is In*

1

**Two sides of the brain,
both used in decision-making**

The right side of our brain is more creative and imaginative; the left processes logic and maps to learned patterns. Both sides influence our choices, but emotion—powered by effective visuals—ultimately drives our decisions.

2

**Business communication is
left brain obsessed**

Data galore. Communication today is overly codified. This closed and narrow approach stymies decisions. Appealing to both the left and right brain—driven by stories, visuals, and data insights—helps us draw implicit meaning from new information, make inferences, and leap beyond our known world.

3

Use data and visuals strategically

Data and visuals are often misused, but they are not the enemy. They're a fantastic way to support your ideas. But they must *always* map directly back to your story.

So, with business storytelling unfluffed, let's now dig in to our storytelling framework and see how it's used in the common, everyday scenarios we all face. You'll be amazed how straightforward it is to flex your story for different audiences. And to make it really stick for you, we've got *tons* of storytelling-in-action examples (both visual and nonvisual) coming up.

Ready to move on?

PART 2

Ok, I'm in—

How Do I Get Started with Business Storytelling?

Getting Started with Business Storytelling

IMAGINE YOUR FAVORITE TV SHOW. Now, think back to that time when—robotically stuffing popcorn in your mouth—you were totally, completely, and utterly absorbed in the story. You weren't bored for a second, and afterwards, you couldn't stop thinking about that *character* or the *creepy house* or the *wrenching conflict*.

Perhaps you're not really sure why the details of *that* story obsessed you so much (more on this later), but from a structural perspective, there is a very good reason why it did:

It took you on a journey

And in fact, all great stories take their audience (viewer/reader/listener) on a journey.

So how exactly did that particular story affect *you* so much, and leave your friend fidgeting on the sofa, sneaking glances at her phone? It's all in the structural details of the story that set up the context, introduced conflict, and sucked you in until the bitter (or hopefully sweet) end.

If the context connects with you, if the characters feel familiar, or if you identify with their journey, your attention is awoken. You want to know how things are going to be resolved. You will remember the story.

ALL GREAT
STORIES TAKE
YOUR AUDIENCE
ON A JOURNEY

Awesome, but what do *context* and *connection* have to do with business storytelling?

Business storytelling is no different than any other type of storytelling. Within every story is a simple framework. Yes, you read that right. Every story contains a simple framework.

And, whether you are the director of *Star Wars,* the author of *War and Peace,* or giving a sales presentation, you are using this framework. And if you're using it well, directing your story to the right audience (more on this in *Chapter 16: Your Audience is Diverse… How Can You Please Everyone?*), then congratulations, you will tell good stories. If you learn to use the framework very well, you will tell great stories and even better, *you're more likely to advance your career.*

PREVIEW

The Story Framework

LET'S TAKE A PEEK UNDER THE HOOD

So what makes a story work?

1

The Four Signposts™

Made up of setting, characters, conflict, and resolution.

2

Your BIG Idea

The #1 take-home message of your story.

3

The WHY-WHAT-HOW

Another helpful way to view the four signposts and your BIG Idea.

Don't panic, *we know*

The story framework has plenty of moving parts. In this section, we will go over the role and the placement of each element, using plenty of examples. Eventually, before you ever put pen to paper, fingers to keyboard, or mouth to phone, you will easily recognize where your facts, data, and ideas fit—or don't fit—within this story framework.

CHAPTER 3

The Four Signposts™

EVERY STORY has four structural elements—or signposts. They are **setting, characters, conflict,** and **resolution.** These signposts create a pattern of ideas that feel familiar, feel human, feel satisfying, but most importantly, *just feel.* And if ideas make us feel, we remember them (refer back to all the cool brain science from *Chapter 1: Meet the Brain Scientists*).

THERE ARE

FOUR BASIC SIGNPOSTS

IN EVERY GREAT STORY

EVERY GREAT STORY HAS
Setting

A setting appears in the opening line of many great stories:

"It was a dark and stormy night..."

"It was a bright cold day in April, and the clocks were striking thirteen."

Or, as nobody who made it through high school can forget:
"It was the best of times, it was the worst of times..."

So what does establishing setting do for stories? And why must it show up so early? The setting gives context that is immediately recognizable to the audience. In traditional storytelling—like movies, books, or plays—this context is often a physical place. But in business storytelling, the setting establishes a current situation, like market climate or a company's overall health.

To establish setting, you can share data and trends that give the audience insight into places or situations where (usually) you've found shortcomings. The context you provide should offer *just enough* information to ensure that your audience has the same baseline understanding of the situation.

Setting builds critical focus

To gain this focus, put up a clear perimeter around these establishing ideas. This gives the context which—to use a well-worn cliché—gets everyone on the same page. It should happen before you get to the meat of your content.

Another way to look at setting is as a "mini-education" that shines the spotlight on those issues that you (and hopefully your audience) care about solving.

In the example below, setting is established as *the state of insurance shopping*. The audience is "placed" in the insurance market, shopping with an agent, online, or from friends/family. The "mini-education" about current purchasing habits brings the focus of the audience to this place—the insurance market setting.

Data provides context to establish the setting of this story →

When *purchasing* or *renewing* insurance, consumers have many **resources** at their fingertips

60% Meet or visit with an agent[1]

71% Research and compare online[2]

80% Get recommendations from friends and family[3]

Do not underestimate the importance of establishing a setting

From the setting, you are ready to advance the story further, eventually toward a solution. But first, you need to show how the context in your story is being experienced by people. *You need characters.*

EVERY GREAT STORY HAS
Characters

We learn to love characters the very first time our parents read us a bedtime story. Curious George, Cinderella, or Winnie the Pooh—these stars of the show are usually the real reason people pay attention to a story. But why is this? Why are characters so irresistible? Simple: because we are human. Characters are human (or at least given human traits and emotions) and "meeting" a character in a story feels familiar to us.

As we observe the emotions characters are experiencing, it triggers a brain response from the right side of our brain. This is where we store language context and facial expressions.[1] And this is what makes us feel something. The characters in your business story should help your audience relate to the situation or problem you present because they see themselves *through* these characters.

Characters serve a critical function in stories

They establish an emotional element. As your audience observes your character's emotional and/or behavioral response to a situation, it elicits their understanding. The more your audience learns about the situation—and the effects it has on your character—the deeper their interest grows. This is the path to advance your story forward.

Who are business characters?

Characters in business storytelling are often portrayed as business participants like customers, suppliers, partners, employees, or key stakeholders.

Whomever it is, you must offer a glimpse of how they are experiencing a business or market condition. This is how your characters will bring your audience a measure of insight and recognition.

In the case of the insurance story example, the characters are *consumers.*

When *purchasing* or *renewing* insurance, consumers have many **resources** at their fingertips

60% Meet or visit with an agent[1]

71% Research and compare online[2]

80% Get recommendations from friends and family[3]

← *Consumers are the characters in this story*

By now you might be thinking: characters? Come on... I'm not a Hollywood screenwriter, I'm an engineer! (or data scientist, or sales associate, or marketing specialist). Right. So let's break this down further to see where this fits into everyone's business world.

Tip!

Don't be afraid to combine setting and characters. In many business communications, these two signposts can blur together to establish context more quickly as one thought or idea. You'll see this reflected in many of the examples throughout this book where one slide contains both the setting and characters of a story vs. separate slides for each signpost.

There are three common ways to introduce a character into any business narrative

A named character

This is an obvious choice, where you would literally invent a fictional persona, give them a name, and place them in your market setting. Let's meet the character "Ben." Like us, he uses his own mobile phone at work. We can relate!

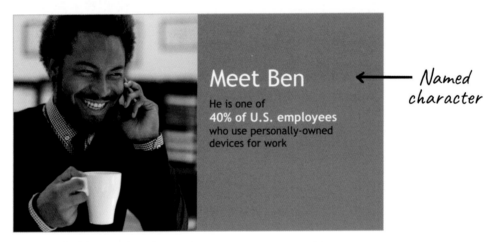

Named character

Unnamed character

Now let's revisit the same story but with an unnamed character. In the same mobile phone example, instead of "Ben" the character(s) are now "U.S. employees." Unnamed characters include broad groups of people whom we don't get to know on a personal level, but can still generally relate to. This is the most common way to introduce characters into business stories because people often feel more comfortable using this approach. There is no right or wrong way to bring in characters; it's just important to have them. If you recall in the insurance story, unnamed characters were also used.

Unnamed character

40%of U.S. employees use personally owned devices at work

You are the character

Finally, you can introduce *yourself* as a character. This is when you might tell a personal story that relates to your overall theme or message. It's commonly done in a keynote speech, TED talk, or some kind of setting where people feel comfortable putting themselves in a story. It's a great way to add emotional appeal to your data and to connect more deeply to your audience.

Ultimately, it's up to you to figure out how to introduce characters into your story. Much will depend on your audience and the type of content you present. Most business storytellers experiment and figure out what works best in different contexts.

Whatever you choose, showing how characters are affected by their setting is critical to building your story, but to really get your audience to care, you need to *up the ante.* You must show that something is happening to your characters. *You need conflict.*

EVERY GREAT STORY HAS
Conflict

Conflict. That sounds so uncomfortable, right? Well, incredibly enough, people not only *don't* find conflict that unpleasant, they actually *crave* it. Just a casual glance at any Oscar, Pulitzer, or Tony (or another fill-in-the-blank prestigious award) shows one clear truth: all great stories have conflict.

Now the nature of the conflict will vary widely. It can be large or small. It can be right in front of you, hidden around the corner, or down the road. But, without some form of conflict or tension, your story has no momentum.

Conflict is a major differentiator between super-exciting and utterly forgettable. Perhaps you have an interesting setting, maybe even a few compelling characters, but without some conflict, it is pretty much a big *"so what?"* Nothing happens... and without, well, *something happening,* there is no potential for growth. There is no reason to move forward to a satisfying resolution.

CONFLICT GIVES YOUR AUDIENCE A REASON TO CARE— A REASON TO LEAN IN.

Lack of conflict in traditional storytelling is boring, but conflict-less business storytelling is not only boring, it's a giant, pointless waste of time. Conflict gives your audience a reason to care—a reason to lean in and listen. *Absence* of a clearly defined conflict is one of the main wastes of meeting time (or unnecessary phone calls or emails). It's why an audience is left wondering: What problem are we trying to solve? Why are we here? This happens every single day in organizations everywhere. *It happens in your organization.*

Conflict is reassuring (and leads to the promised land)

But, before you get anxious (all this conflict talk might be reminding you of that last wearisome argument you had with your toddler/ teenager), know that conflict in business storytelling is not only interesting, it's reassuring. Your audience—whether a boss, customer, or colleague—can see that you understand a meaningful problem. Better yet, they can see that your facts, data, and ideas show you understand *their* problem (and are on the path to resolving it).

Think about an executive's world. They're inundated with problems. But they know that hidden problems are much scarier than visible ones. It's only when a problem has been identified that they can begin to solve it.

REVEALING CONFLICT IN YOUR STORY LETS YOU BE A HERO TWICE— FIRST WHEN YOU IDENTIFY A PROBLEM, AND THEN AGAIN WHEN YOU PROPOSE A WAY TO FIX IT.

The conflict equation—a deeper look

Conflict is so critical to business storytelling that it's worth defining further. Inherent in the description of conflict, is that the situation you describe is current. It's happening right now and is today's "old," entrenched story. The main cause of the discord is that this current situation is blocking opportunity or the possibility of a better future. Any conflict should pinpoint where incongruity or inadequacy of the current situation exists.

A classic business conflict is the activity of competitors. Imagine telling the C-Suite of your security company, who has been happy just targeting small businesses for years, that their main competitor is gaining big market share with larger companies. You want these executives to wake up and see they are ignoring a valuable market segment. You want to show them that their attachment to a familiar marketing pattern—the status quo—could spell trouble in the future. To get them to change their strategy, *they must feel the tension.*

The path to killing status quo is conflict

Leaders may tend to get attached to what's familiar. They can cling to the status quo when they don't have a better alternative. Conflict plays a critical role in changing their mindset. Because when you successfully build conflict, you have a window of opportunity to suggest something better.

Introducing conflict is a status quo killer.

The conflict escalation strategy

One interesting way to bring conflict into your story is to introduce it as a series of small conflicts that build up and up and up into a much larger conflict. In the insurance story example, the first slide introduces

Current Situation
(Old Story)

Opportunity/Better Future
(New Story)

conflict, highlighting how complex the insurance purchasing process is. In the next slide, the conflict escalates to show how—currently—the future looks bleak for reaching the next generation of insurance shoppers. This is an example of a classic business conflict—old methods of doing business aren't working anymore. (Note: these conflict slides are part of a larger narrative that's already been established with setting and characters. For this full insurance story, see *Chapter 6: Putting It All Together.*)

Conflict introduced here

Conflict escalates here

Once conflict is established, move on quickly

Great business storytelling is like a recipe, and you are the chef. Take care not to over- or under-pepper your story with conflict. With your setting, you are shining the light on a certain market situation. With your characters, you are establishing how a person or people are experiencing this situation. And with introduction of conflict, you are illuminating a current problem. And if you have done your job, you've revealed shortcomings in the comfortable, old status quo. But you haven't given them the alternative... yet. These first three signposts have put your audience in a mentally uncomfortable place. *Good. You've done your job.*

Great business storytellers know how much conflict is enough to secure attention—and concern—but not overdo it. Piling on the conflict can be off-putting at best, insulting at worst. With the right mix of setting, characters, and conflict, you will find that contextual sweet spot. You are ready to offer the crucial payoff your audience is craving: *the resolution.*

THE FIRST THREE SIGNPOSTS PUT YOUR AUDIENCE IN A MENTALLY UNCOMFORTABLE PLACE. *GOOD.* YOU'VE DONE YOUR JOB.

EVERY GREAT STORY HAS
Resolution

The resolution brings your characters—and your audience—safely through the conflict. *Phew!* You may now unveil the new opportunity that will take the organization on the path to a rosier future.

So what does a resolution look like in a business story? It's the nitty-gritty, the "meat and potatoes" of your narrative. For a salesperson, it's the features and benefits of their product or solution. For a consultant, it's the direct approach (and timeline) for solving a problem. For a product manager giving an update, it's the recommendations to spur product growth.

Here's how we **build relevance** with tomorrow's shoppers

SIMPLIFY
the discovery process

PERSONALIZE
the customer experience

DIFFERENTIATE
our product offerings

This is the resolution

In the case of the insurance company concerned with reaching the next generation of shoppers, the resolution is a strategy to reach these new consumers. It directly addresses the previously stated conflict (a murky buying process). The resolution is to simplify, personalize, and clarify product offerings. After this, a series of follow-on slides can address these solutions in greater detail. (Note: Hang tight! The next chapter shows how this entire insurance story flows from beginning to end using all four signposts.)

Which signpost do most of us usually start with?

If you guessed resolution, you are correct. We all want to get there fast. But moving speedily doesn't mean you should start with your resolution. *Because starting with resolution is the opposite of good business storytelling.*

In the insurance story, the resolution would have had much different meaning if it had come first. The audience would surely be skeptical about *why* they need to "build relevance with tomorrow's shoppers," unless they understood that their current methods were beginning to fail.

Can you imagine if *The Wizard of Oz* started with "There's no place like home"? Why should we care if some little Kansan girl finds her way home? Well, we wouldn't unless we saw her get lost in a tornado, find friends and scary creatures, then ultimately meet a fake wizard. We care because we went on the journey with Dorothy. The resolution was earned.

In business communications, we are so quick to talk about ourselves—typically our solution/product/company—that we skip the whole part about building context. We forget to tell anyone why it matters.

But wait, I don't always get the luxury of time

Many of us feel the stress of an impatient audience (see *Chapter 15: You've Got Five Minutes with an Executive… Go!*). We believe we need to *hurry up* and make our point quickly. But telling a business story does not mean you force your audience to waste their time. Yes, you should get to your point quickly, but moving with speed does not mean starting with your resolution.

You must always build context for your audience—including some healthy tension—so they have a reason to care. Otherwise, they will not be motivated to hear the details of your resolution.

Your resolution must be earned.

MOVING WITH SPEED DOES NOT MEAN STARTING WITH YOUR RESOLUTION.

The **birth order** of your signposts *matters*

The first three signposts of storytelling—setting, characters, and conflict—can be introduced in any order. In fact, many stories start with conflict before we have zeroed in on any characters or established setting.

Imagine how many movies start with someone running from something dangerous! You think: Who is that guy? Where is he? Who is chasing him? *Why can't I stop watching this?* Conflict first is a storytelling device that can work well.

And the same is true in a business narrative. You can start with characters, then move to setting, and on to conflict (or any variation of this order) but again, the resolution must always come last.

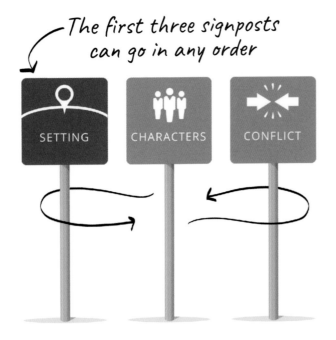

The first three signposts can go in any order

SETTING   CHARACTERS   CONFLICT

RESOLUTION

The resolution must always come last in your story

A LOOK AHEAD

The four signposts viewed through a different lens

So, you've got your four signposts of storytelling—cool, right? We think so. But, we also know that many of you might still need more convincing. You can't stop imagining what your audience might be thinking as they take in your story: *come on... get to your point already.*

We hear you. But hang tight. Let's take a look at these signposts in a slightly different way. Let's delve deeper into the underlying role each one plays within your story—and why each one is integral in moving it forward. This will help you fully understand how the parts of the framework work together to build up your message and ultimately, sell your ideas.

CHAPTER 4

The WHY, WHAT, and HOW of Business Storytelling

ANOTHER HELPFUL WAY to identify and prioritize which of your facts, data, or ideas to include—and in what order—is to make sure that *everything* brings either a WHY, a WHAT, or a HOW to your story

Your WHY is your setting, characters, and conflict

The first three signposts are the WHY of your story. Specifically, this is where you lay out ideas, data, and insights to establish WHY anyone should care about your resolution. Your WHY can be presented either verbally or visually in 30 seconds, 60 seconds, or longer, depending on how much time you have. So yes, you will be able to deliver your WHY to your Uber co-passenger *and* get him caring about your innovative product idea, all in five minutes.

Your HOW is your resolution

If you've clearly established your WHY, you've (hopefully) given your (trapped) car companion a reason to care. But the ride is ending soon! You're nearly there and you must move *quickly* to your resolution. This is the HOW of your story. This is how *your* new service, solution, or product is going to solve a problem—the conflict—that you hope you have made him care about.

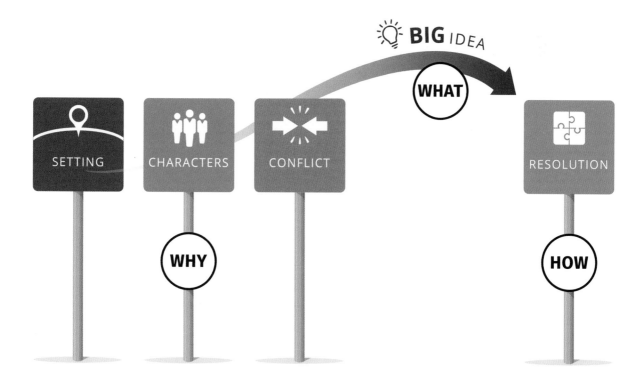

But wait... not so fast

There is still one last thing you must do before jumping to your resolution. (Yikes, the ride is almost over!) There is another key message, integral to every compelling story, that you need to state before your resolution. It's the seed which will ultimately blossom into the idea that you want your prospect to take with him after he hops out of the car.

Your WHAT is your BIG Idea

Every great story needs a **BIG Idea.** Your BIG Idea is the one thing you want your audience to remember (because they won't remember everything). This is the WHAT of your story.

Despite your lack of time in this—and many other—business situations, you absolutely need a BIG Idea. And here's why: when you successfully introduce conflict—when you've made your audience care—you are causing discomfort. They are thinking: *"Wow, I see. That's definitely a problem!"* This is when you have done everything right.

But now they are craving some immediate relief from that discomfort. They need one further mental *bridge* to help bring them through the conflict and help them accept your resolution.

Your BIG Idea is what will satisfy that craving, It will feel good... and right. And because of that, they will remember it.

YOU NEED A BIG IDEA—THE ONE THING YOU WANT YOUR AUDIENCE TO REMEMBER (BECAUSE THEY WON'T REMEMBER EVERYTHING).

YOUR AUDIENCE NEEDS

A MENTAL BRIDGE

TO HELP BRING THEM

THROUGH THE CONFLICT AND

ACCEPT YOUR RESOLUTION

(THAT'S YOUR BIG IDEA)

CHAPTER 5

Your BIG Idea

THE BIG IDEA IS IMPORTANT, so let's dig a little deeper. What *exactly* is a BIG Idea? Because you might be thinking, wait, I have *many* big ideas. Yes, you do. But in the business stories you tell, there should be only one, thematic BIG Idea that's an inspiring, insightful, and *actionable* preview of what's to come in your story. Another way to look at it is that it's the "trailer" before the movie with tantalizing flashes of the key scenes. *You're basically saying, "I've got this, stay with me, it's coming..."*

But I'm so close! Why can't I just get to the punchline?

In a great story, you've established context. You've built in some uncomfortable conflict. You've gotten your audience to care. But a well-crafted narrative offers a captivating and insightful BIG Idea that keeps your audience with you through to the end. Your BIG Idea is the one thing you want your audience to remember.

YOUR BIG IDEA IS A SIMPLE,

CONVERSATIONAL STATEMENT

THAT CAPTURES THE

WHAT OF YOUR STORY

WITH HIGH-LEVEL BENEFITS

Examples of BIG Ideas

Here are some examples of BIG Ideas in business that can be expressed verbally or visually. Notice how they're short, concise, and don't contain jargon. Look for a deeper exploration of how to construct a BIG Idea in *Chapter 8: A Simple Path to Building Your BIG Idea.*

We need to invest more in programs aimed at keeping our top talent

A new comp structure will help us recover our margins

Let's partner to reinvent our supply chain process

To scale our global business, we must get intentional about cross-border shoppers

You need a safe space to protect your business on every employee's device

Now, let's revisit our insurance story from earlier. After establishing the WHY (the future looks bleak for reaching the next generation of insurance shoppers), but before unveiling the HOW, this story offers a BIG Idea:

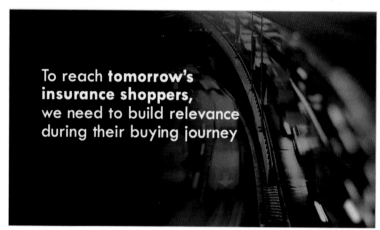

To reach **tomorrow's insurance shoppers,** we need to build relevance during their buying journey

This is a BIG Idea

This BIG Idea is the hint of what's to come in the resolution, which will be a series of strategies and tactics to *build* that relevance. Like in this example, people will notice how simple it is at first glance—and it's reassuring. Rather than pivoting from your conflict with a detailed chart or a page filled with bullet points, a simple statement like this with a thematic background photo eases the audience into your nitty-gritty details. It's simple and memorable.

IN SHORT...

So whether you have one minute, five minutes, or 30 minutes, you should always take the time to establish the WHY of your business story, unleash your BIG Idea (the WHAT), and then move powerfully into your resolution (the HOW). This will ensure your message is absorbed and remembered well after that brief Uber ride, that power lunch, or that critical virtual meeting. *Every time.*

CHAPTER 6

Putting It All Together: Sample Story

YOU NOW KNOW that good stories *always* include a WHY, WHAT, and HOW. Let's take a bird's-eye view of what this looks like by revisiting our insurance story and seeing all the story elements in their proper flow. First, some more background: GO Insurance is a trusted home and auto insurance brand that's been passed down

01

02

03

―Setting & Characters―   ――Conflict――

07
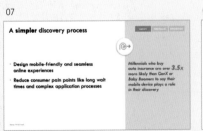

08
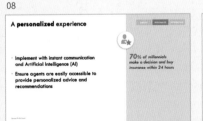

09

――Resolution――

through families for 55 years. But, if they want to *stay* in the family, they'll have to adjust to the habits of Millennials and Gen Zs, who purchase insurance differently than Mom and Grandma.

This story begins with a clear WHY. The insurance buying setting is introduced along with its characters—the consumers—showing how they purchase insurance. Conflict moves in, explaining the *complexity* of the insurance purchase, then escalates with data showing that the old road to reach new consumers is disappearing. Then the WHAT (BIG Idea) is revealed, explaining that GO must build relevance with tomorrow's shoppers. And finally, the HOW (the resolution) clearly lays out the details. The restated BIG Idea finishes it off, ending the story on-message.

04

Conflict

05

BIG Idea

06

Resolution

10

BIG Idea

This story came in the form of a ten-slide presentation. But remember, business stories come in all shapes and sizes. Keep on reading for more examples.

RECAP

The Baseline Story Structure

ALL TOGETHER NOW, FOLKS

And so you have it. We've unpacked the individual elements
that make up a well-constructed story. Let's take one more
look at the baseline story structure.

1

The four signposts

Every story should have four
signposts (setting, characters,
conflict, and resolution).

2

First three signposts must come first

The order of signposts matters.
The first three signposts are the
openers (in any order that makes
sense). They explain WHY anyone
should care about your story and can
be expressed verbally or visually.

3

Have a BIG Idea

What's the one thing you want
your audience to remember?
Your BIG Idea should be a simple,
conversational statement that
captures the WHAT of your story.

4

Bring relief with your BIG Idea

After introducing conflict in your story, offer some relief. Bring in your BIG Idea to address the conflict and *preview* what's to come in your resolution.

5

Finally, reveal your resolution

The fourth signpost, your resolution, details the HOW of your features, solution, or recommendation.

PART 3

Thanks, got the basics.

What Else Can Help Me?

CHAPTER 7

Push Your Story Forward with Active Headlines

CONGRATULATIONS. You now have the basic building blocks of a well-crafted story. You've even seen a real business story *in action.* It showed the WHY (the setting, characters, and conflict), the WHAT (the BIG Idea), and finally, the HOW (the resolution) of the story. Be sure to bookmark *Chapter 6: Putting It All Together* as a helpful reference. For even more examples of how storytelling works in business communications, check out all of *Part 4: Let's See the Magic! How Does Storytelling Show Up in Everyday Business?*

You're now ready to take it to the next level. So, with these basic components in place, let's apply a *power tool* that guarantees to propel your story forward.

Introducing: Active headlines

Whether you're communicating a one-page overview, an email, or presentation slides, **headlines** elevate your most consequential ideas above all the rest. Headlines achieve three important things: they channel audience focus, help you control the narrative, and ensure your story is moving forward. They might sound complicated, but if you've ever read a magazine or newspaper, you're already well acquainted with them. *Every* news story—from *The New York Times* to *Forbes* to *Fast Company*—uses a headline to grab readers' attention by advertising what the article is about up front.

HEADLINES ARE
CONVERSATIONAL STATEMENTS
THAT CAPTURE YOUR INSIGHT
AND HELP ADVANCE A STORY

LIKE ANY NEWS STORY, YOUR HEADLINE SHOULD PULL OUT THE KEY IDEA OR INSIGHT AND PUT IT RIGHT ON TOP.

Slide decks offer a great example of how headlines advance a story. The title of every slide is an opportunity for a powerful headline. And all together, they perform a kind of relay race. Each slide headline passes the story "baton" onto the next slide headline. Flowing from one to another (through each of the signposts), they advance the story to the "finish line."

And *this* is why headlines are so incredibly important. Their strong contextual—and visual—signal shows your audience where you are in the narrative and where you are about to go. Just like with any juicy news article headline, it gives a reader/viewer/listener a strong enticement, pulling them toward what you want to tell them next.

Headlines are super-useful (so what's up with vague headings everywhere?)

Even though it's clear that headlines signal attention like a lighthouse beacon signals boats, and move stories along like the baton in an Olympic relay race, business folks *often* don't use them. Instead, they use vague, passive **headings.**

To understand the crucial difference between headlines and headings, think about a slide deck. A slide title heading often shows up as *Next*

Steps, Revenue, or the most quintessentially boring heading: *Update.* We've all seen them. Yes, these headings are large, bolded words dominating other words or images. But they are unhelpful. They do absolutely nothing to illuminate the *newsworthiness* of the slide. They don't move the story forward. And worst of all, they force people to work harder than they need to, to decode your message.

Headings are a terrible waste of prime real estate.

But before you put on your journalist hat and begin crafting active slide headlines, let's see what your collection of headlines looks like from 30,000 feet. What's the significance of how they fit together? (Hint: It's *very* significant.)

Active headlines outline your entire story

One of the most impressive skills of great communicators is how they knit their ideas, facts, and data together and make them flow. They take their audience on a journey. Well, guess what?

Active headlines are like the "GPS roadmap" of your story's journey.

Once you've identified the key story elements, building headlines is the next step. What's incredible is that when you string them together, you've got your complete narrative outline. How do you know you've done it right? Just review each headline *alone,* without additional content or visuals. Do they recognizably move your story forward? Do they create a story with momentum? If so, you've completed the outline of your story. You've got your roadmap; now you can start to fill in the rest of your ideas.

What's more, once you have developed your outline, your headlines become a crucial guide for everyone involved in the meeting.

ACTIVE HEADLINES ARE THE ORGANIZATIONAL FRAMEWORK FOR YOUR STORY.

When your audience is lost, headlines orient them

It cannot be overstated how much active headlines keep your audience on the narrative journey with you. Imagine this common scenario:

You sneak into the conference room (or virtual meeting) ten minutes late. The first five (stressful) minutes are a scramble to figure out what you missed. Being late is one thing, but appearing *out of the loop* is embarrassing.

Yikes! What did I miss? Where are we in the story? Did the presenter already share an important detail?

If the story isn't immediately clear to you—as your eyes desperately scan the slides—it's probably because of passive headings like *Q1 Update, Agenda,* or *Market Size.* They tell you nothing. But information-rich headlines like *Q1 Showed a Huge Turnaround from the Previous Two Quarters* allows you to jump right in.

Headlines orient the storyteller (yes, that's you)

Stories get derailed all the time. They get derailed when you're facing an impatient executive who demands you skip ahead. They get derailed when your co-presenting teammate goes off on a tangent. They get derailed when the lunch cart arrives. No one benefits more from having a GPS than the storyteller. Headlines will keep you on track and nimble in the face of an unpredictable audience (and what audience isn't?).

Bottom line: headlines are simple, clever prompts that help you tell your story, stay in control, appear polished, and always find your way back to the narrative trail.

A playbook for writing great headlines

You can always be creative with your headlines, but they must also serve their primary purpose of advancing your story. Good headlines are concise, specific, and conversational.

Here are a few tips for writing strong headlines:

Be concise

Keep it brief and eliminate unnecessary words. Edit! Edit! Edit!

Be specific

Include a key data point, element of time, or unit of measure that means something to your audience.

Be conversational

Say your headlines aloud—they should sound natural and avoid jargon. If you're stuck, imagine that your slides or email could talk on their own. What would they say?

Headlines first, visuals second

For any visual story you build—whether it's an executive summary, presentation deck, or one-page overview—build your headlines *before* you build your visuals. This is because your headlines, which serve as the outline of your story, should directly drive your choice of visuals. So sure, feel free to jot down ideas, but it's best to frame out your headlines first before designing anything. (Heads up: great ideas for visuals are coming in *Chapter 9: Five Well-Tested Ways to Visualize Your Story.)*

Presto! Let's transform some headings into headlines

We've talked up headlines. We've railed against unfortunate headings. Let's see how different they look in our everyday business communications. On the left, you'll see vague headings that basically tell us nothing. On the right, we've transformed them into newsworthy, active headlines that make us want to lean in and know more. See the difference?

Heading	Headline
Revenues	Revenues skyrocket over 3 years after cloud launch
Update	Project X on track for Q4 go-live
Timeline	We expect roll-out to occur in 3 phases
Consumer Behavior	Most consumers buy or switch mobile devices during the holidays
Implementation Timeline	Trends show 3-to-6-month implementation timeline is accurate

A word about word count

Now let's address the elephant in the room. Yes, a headline contains more words than a heading. That's because a headline needs to pack in more information. It tells your audience *precisely* what they need to know or do with the information you're sharing. So there's a trade-off. You're making your audience read *more* words in the slide title (or email subject line or written proposal, etc.) but those words add huge meaning to the story. Anyone is grateful—relieved even—if you give them real, valuable *meat* instead of filler.

Incorporate headlines into all of your business communications and you'll never waste valuable slide real estate, that coveted email subject line, or a verbal transition again.

Pack your words with meaning, drive curiosity, and push your story forward.

It's worth it.

Building headlines from your story framework

Let's revisit our storytelling framework to help guide the construction of great headlines. Below are several examples of "starter" headlines that map to each of the four signposts (for BIG Idea headline examples, see *Chapter 8: A Simple Path to Building Your BIG Idea*).

ANYONE IS GRATEFUL WHEN
THEY DON'T HAVE TO SQUINT
AND LEAN IN TO UNDERSTAND
THE SIGNIFICANCE OF
YOUR CONTENT

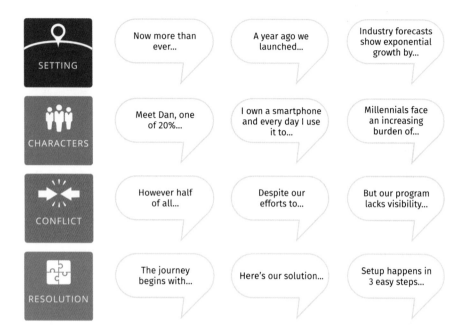

Notice how the language used in each headline is appropriate for its respective signpost? The headlines used in the setting of a story are neutral in tone. The headlines linked to the characters of a story are people-driven, describing a population the audience is meant to relate to. And the headlines used to describe the conflict have a tone of tension and negativity. They include words like "however," "despite," and "but" to indicate the narrative shift.

IN SHORT...

Active headlines are a vital storytelling tool

So there you have it. Active headlines are your power tool and GPS roadmap for storytelling. Include a headline for every chart, diagram, or bulleted list you display. Include a headline as the subject line of any email you send. Include verbal "headlines" for any virtual meeting you lead. *Headlines should drive every business conversation.*

CHAPTER 8

A Simple Path to Building Your BIG Idea

YOUR STORYTELLING TOOLKIT IS GROWING.

Let's take a deeper look at the BIG Idea concept we introduced in *Chapter 5: Your BIG Idea*. Your BIG Idea is the heart and soul of every story you tell. It must be captivating and insightful.

EVERY FACT, IDEA, OR PIECE OF DATA YOU INCLUDE IN YOUR STORY—NO MATTER HOW MINOR—MUST CONNECT TO YOUR BIG IDEA. *EVERYTHING.*

And so, with the fate of your story largely resting on your BIG Idea, let's explore further what it is and how to make it powerful. Here are four key characteristics:

Four critical characteristics of a BIG Idea

1. Your BIG Idea should address the conflict in your story

The first three signposts of your story (setting, characters, and conflict) are the foundation for your story—and they're very important. Remember, this is *why* your audience will care about your presented problem (your conflict). If you don't make them care about your conflict, they won't care about your resolution.

Once you've established the first three signposts, you must reassure your audience that there is a way to address this problem. *This is your BIG Idea.*

Your BIG Idea and your conflict are like a yin/yang scenario. They belong together. If you can't figure out what your BIG Idea is, it's probably because your story doesn't have a clear conflict. Look for this important signal *early on* in your story development.

2. Your BIG Idea should provide insight

The most powerful BIG Ideas are filled with great promise. This hint of the future should give your audience an inspiring *preview* of a newer, better opportunity. Back in *Chapter 2: Data (Yes, Sometimes Overused) Is Not the Villain,* we examined insights and how they shift us toward a brighter future. This is precisely the role your BIG Idea performs. It's the *granddaddy* of every other insight in your narrative. And like any good insight, it should transform your audience's thinking—and shift their mindset—to where *you* need it to be.

3. Your BIG Idea should be actionable

Your BIG Idea is also where your insights become actionable. You have brought your audience on a journey through the first three signposts of storytelling. Every new insight is built upon the ones before, to enhance their understanding of a present situation or problem. And when you tell them enough to bring them to the edge, it begs the question: *What's next?*

THE BIG IDEA IS A TURNING POINT WHERE YOUR INSIGHTS BECOME A CALL TO ACTION.

Your audience needs to know *in one simple statement* what they should know or do. And if you get it right, they'll curiously lean in to learn the details of your plan (the resolution).

4. Your BIG Idea should focus completely on your audience

This is an important one (and is often difficult). Your audience will only buy into a BIG Idea that is focused on them and their needs. So how can you restrain yourself from talking about, well, *yourself?* Try this: *never* include your company or product name in your BIG Idea (this can be especially challenging for salespeople.) A powerful BIG Idea is never about one product or one company. It is *always* about the larger concept behind it all.

The larger concept is what decision-makers care about.

Come on... let's build a BIG Idea

Ready to roll up your sleeves and craft a BIG Idea? Here's what you need to know. Your BIG Idea is made up of two parts:

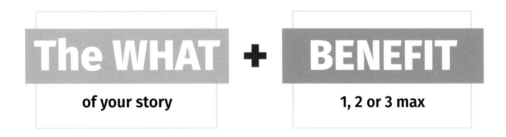

Your BIG Idea is a concise, specific, and conversational statement that encapsulates the WHAT of your story plus a few high-level benefits.

Remember, your BIG Idea must inspire your audience and directly address the conflict of your story. But it also has another job. It should *preview* your forthcoming resolution by touching on a few (just a few) high-level benefits. We suggest no more than three.

Like your headlines, your BIG Idea should easily flow. To test for this, always say your BIG Idea aloud (like you're telling it to a friend). Does it immediately make sense? Does is sound conversational? Does it roll off your tongue?

Let's see some BIG Ideas in action—based on a real company—from one we call Nirvana Tech.

CASE STUDY

But first, some context

Nirvana Tech services airports and schedules around-the-clock technician support to ensure all screens at airports are working properly. Alex Fuente is the Senior Director of Technical Support at Nirvana Tech and has been given the opportunity to present to the CFO. Alex wants to recommend and get the CFO to approve a new compensation structure for Nirvana's service technicians because he's noticed that the company's margins are eroding during the late-night hours. He has 15 minutes to make his case and get approval.

To address the problem, Alex must first make the case for WHY the company is a) losing money and b) has an inefficient compensation structure (causing loss of margins). The BIG Idea comes next.

Here are three variations of how Alex could craft the BIG Idea. Notice how the *order* of the WHAT and BENEFIT doesn't matter as long they both directly address the conflict of the story.

VARIATION #1	A new comp structure will help recover our margins
VARIATION #2	We need a new comp structure to recover our margins
VARIATION #3	To recover our margins, we need a new comp structure

WHAT   BENEFIT

BIG Ideas can be soundbites (but they don't have to be)

What do we mean by a soundbite? BIG Idea soundbites are *even more conversational* than a typical WHAT + BENEFIT statement because they scale down the number of elements. They contain the WHAT part, but not a BENEFIT. Also, soundbites are often expressed verbally because they easily roll off the tongue. They contain language that feels colloquial and familiar. Good ones are easy for your audience to repeat well after your meeting or presentation ends.

Caution: Only use a BIG Idea soundbite if it comes naturally

Soundbites are not a requirement and should *never* be forced. For a soundbite to work as your BIG Idea, it must clearly reinforce your original WHAT + BENEFIT statement, support it, and ultimately communicate your BIG Idea in an even more conversational way. Again, if it works, great... but don't spend hours on it.

Here are some more examples of BIG Ideas:

BIG Idea (WHAT + BENEFIT)	BIG Idea Soundbite (optional)
We need to implement the performance tracking dashboard to improve business results	Let's hit the "go button"
Embracing sustainability will help us meet customer demands and protect our leadership position	It's time to "go green"

WHAT   BENEFIT

Notice how BIG Idea soundbites only include a WHAT (no BENEFIT)

Get inspired by these prompts

Your BIG Idea is the underpinning of your entire message. And remember, to make it sound natural, use your "speaking" voice not your "writing" voice to develop it. Here are some BIG Idea prompts to give you some inspiration:

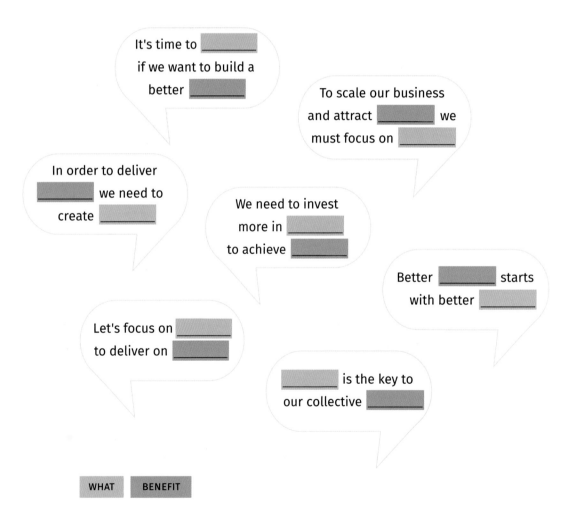

Your BIG Idea checklist

Let's sum up your BIG Idea. Here are the *fundamental* differences between a weak and a strong BIG Idea:

Weak	Strong
✗ Wordy	✓ Concise
✗ Includes jargon and/or unfamiliar acronyms	✓ Conversational (uses everyday language)
✗ Does not include the WHAT of your story	✓ Includes the WHAT of your story
✗ Benefits are not clear, too many	✓ Benefits are clear (1, 2, or 3 max)
✗ Difficult to remember and share with others	✓ Easy to remember and share with others
✗ Audience is not compelled to ask "how" or "tell me more"	✓ Audience is compelled to lean in and ask "how" or "tell me more"
✗ Doesn't flow easily from your setting/character/conflict to resolution	✓ Flows easily from your setting/character/conflict to resolution

IN SHORT...

By now you've learned about basic story structure, seen active headlines in action, and been shown how to craft your BIG Idea. With all that in the bag, you are ready to take your storytelling up a notch. Let's explore some tried and true ways (with loads of examples) to bring it all to life visually.

CHAPTER 9

Five Well-Tested Ways to Visualize Your Story

WE LIVE IN A VISUAL WORLD. Highway billboards, TV commercials, and nonstop social media newsfeeds constantly barrage us with messages. But, if you take a closer look, the visuals you remember aren't just built to be randomly colorful or pretty.

CLEVER VISUALS ARE HIGHLY STRATEGIC—THEY GET US TO NOTICE AND TAKE ACTION.

And this same logic directly applies to business communications. Well-designed visuals amplify our insights and recommendations, so they're easily understood, better remembered, and more likely to spur action.

Why do visuals help us remember things?

As John Medina told us in *Chapter 1: Meet the Brain Scientists,* neuroscience has everything to do with why we remember visuals more than the spoken word or reading text. He found that an idea expressed in visual form is processed much faster than the same information either printed or spoken. Visuals can humanize your ideas, which trigger emotions and feelings. And it's emotion (even more than pure logic) that motivates us into action.

Conversely, distracting or boring visuals (such as pages or screens filled with pure text or numbers) will dull our emotions and slow decision-making down.

Unfortunately, business communication is afflicted with terrible visuals. It is mired in text, charts, and bullet points. To understand why getting visuals right is so important, you must ask yourself one question: *What is the purpose of my presentation? Or email? Or proposal?* Is it to get a decision made or move a business conversation forward?

Why the best-laid plans for visuals go *terribly* wrong

Visuals usually go wrong for two main reasons: we lack a) time or b) a story strategy to guide us. Let's talk about time first. We are completely aware that everybody wants to save time, reuse, and repurpose existing content. We know. And we've all thrown together slides from old decks or "borrowed" slides from a co-worker to cross that finish line quickly. Initially, this always seems to save time. But it's usually at the expense of a coherent deck. Why is this? Because it is very difficult to build a coherent deck without first developing a story strategy. The story strategy offers the needed framework that dictates everything that should be included in the story... and everything that shouldn't.

WHEN YOU ASSEMBLE A DECK WITHOUT MINDFULNESS, INTENT, OR A STORY STRATEGY, YOUR MESSAGE OFTEN GETS LOST.

Frankendecks (when bad visuals happen to good people)

We have a very technical term for this type of incoherent, hodge-podge communication. We call it a *Frankendeck™*. You've seen them. *Frankendecks* show up in our meetings and flood our inbox. And the results can be scary! Your audience is left confused. There's no clear message or call to action. And ultimately, you've missed an opportunity to influence a decision and drive business forward.

Bad visuals are everywhere in the business world. Data, bullets, and text are horribly overused; colors, fonts, and images often seem random. And let's not even talk about the endless, cheesy stock photography.

So, how can we get our visuals right?

A visual toolkit (just for you)

You understand that strong visuals are absolutely critical for a strong message. So let's get into five well-tested ways to visualize your story. Everything we will explore—photos, diagrams, data, text, and video—are commonly used to advance a story.

Photo

Photos can be truly powerful in storytelling. Pictures are infinitely more memorable than text because they humanize your message and help connect it to your audience on an emotional level. Photos are also useful in creating a mood or theme for your presentation— particularly if you are presenting data or facts about *people*.

Diagram

Diagrams are great for "chunking out" and clustering information into small, digestible concepts using various shapes and colors. Diagrams can be a great alternative to overused charts and tables, even timelines, to grab attention, and call out your key message.

Data

Data is most often presented in the form of traditional charts, graphs, and tables. However, don't be afraid to *think outside the chart* by using a combination of oversized numbers, text, and basic shapes to draw the eye to a key data insight and advance a story forward.

Text

Yes, text is a type of visual!
In fact, it's the most common
visual. And unfortunately,
it's grossly overused. Since
popular programs like
PowerPoint default to bullets
and text, we often get slides
that are jammed up with
words, making it difficult
to quickly scan and digest.
But text can work very well
when used sparingly with
contrasting color and size.

Video

Video is an excellent way
to change the pace, the
voice, and the medium of
any business story. Video can
help set the tone for your
story's opening, bring your
characters to life, or provide
a dramatic close that
reinforces your BIG Idea.
It's best kept brief and, of
course, totally on message.
It's also important that you
easily get in and out of your
video so as not to disrupt the
overall flow of your story.

Visual guidelines to support your story structure

You have five options for visualizing your story. Now let's layer on some guidelines for how these visuals fit into the baseline story structure. To review, these include the four signposts: setting, characters, conflict, and resolution. (Another way to look at this structure is through the lens of WHY, WHAT, and HOW.) And finally, there's the BIG Idea driving it all home. Keep in mind, these visuals are options for different business stories. These are not, however, hard-and-fast rules.

For the WHY of your story (setting, characters, conflict),
you're more likely to use photos, oversized text, or metrics.

WHAT

Photo   Text

For the WHAT of your story (your BIG Idea), large text statements work well to really make it stand out. You can certainly include a textured background or photo, but this is not critical.

RESOLUTION

HOW

Diagram   Data   Text   Video

For the HOW of your story (resolution), you'll likely want to use diagrams, data, text, and video to bring the details of your story to life.

Always select a good balance of visuals

There is no exact science to selecting the right mix of visuals, but it's a good idea to offer a decent variety. We always advise never to fall in love with any one photo, chart, or diagram. Always be mindful of your story first, then select visuals (that directly support your story) second.

Here are some other best practices to consider:

Don't be repetitive

If one visual category seems to dominate your story—too many photos, text slides, tables, etc.—rethink your choices and look for ways to mix things up.

Keep it simple

You don't need to use every visual display. On the flip side, don't feel obligated to use too many different visual displays. And don't be afraid to use a visual approach that's new to you.

Text is okay in moderation

Slides crowded with text are difficult for your audience to take in. However, sometimes it is okay to use *just* text. We favor using text in a short, declarative statement *by itself* as a brief, powerful "visual pause." Remember, *less is always more*.

Extreme makeovers: Slide edition!

You've learned the anatomy of the BIG Idea, how to use active headlines to push your story forward, and finally, the five most common visualization techniques that'll bring your story to life. But, as that endless flood of popular reality shows prove, nothing highlights the difference between a disastrous "hot mess" and a design triumph more than—drum roll please—*the extreme makeover.*

So buckle up and behold eight extreme slide makeovers. You'll see where the bad slides went bad. You'll see where the great slides really soar. Seven powerful examples will show you how to give your audience exactly what they need to *know* and *do* in just a glance. And hopefully, this will remind you that simple, clear, magnetic visuals never appear by accident.

MINDFULNESS IN CHOOSING YOUR VISUALS IS A KEY DRIVER FOR SUCCESSFUL STORYTELLING.

A LOOK AHEAD

When you turn the page you'll find the **top half** of the page shows the classic "before and after" slides—no markup. The **bottom half** of the page shows what's *not* working with the "before," and what *is* working with the "after." (For fun, cover the bottom half of each page and try to guess what's wrong and right with each slide. Can you tell?)

Video gaming stats

- There are 2.7 billion active video gamers around the world
- Of the total U.S. gaming population, 45% consists of female gamers
- Young adults between 26-35 years of age spend over 8 hours per week playing video games

Source: State of Online Gaming, Limelight Networks

BEFORE *What's not working?*

Title is a → heading (vague)

Data is buried in a list, hard to scan

Video gaming stats

- There are 2.7 billion active video gamers around the world
- Of the total U.S. gaming population, 45% consists of female gamers
- Young adults between 26-35 years of age spend over 8 hours per week playing video games

Source: State of Online Gaming, Limelight Networks

Photos are inconsistent in style and alignment

The video gaming industry shows no signs of slowing down

2.7B
Active video gamers around the world

45%
of the U.S. gaming population is female

8 hours+
Time per week 26-35-year-olds spend playing video games

Source: State of Online Gaming, Limelight Networks

AFTER *What's working?*

Title is a headline (concise, specific, conversational)

The video gaming industry shows no signs of slowing down

2.7B
Active video gamers around the world

45%
of the U.S. gaming population is female

8 hours+
Time per week 26-35-year-olds spend playing video games

Source: State of Online Gaming, Limelight Networks

← Oversized metrics make data quick and easy to digest

Photos are consistent in style and alignment

Client relationships

- Social media connections
  - Connect and maintain rapport on Linked In or Twitter
- Check-in calls
  - Remain involved and informed with clear, open communication
- Face-to-face meetings
  - Foster relationships and connect on a deeper level

BEFORE *What's not working?*

Title is a
heading
(vague)

Client relationships

- Social media connections
  - Connect and maintain rapport on Linked In or Twitter
- Check-in calls
  - Remain involved and informed with clear, open communication
- Face-to-face meetings
  - Foster relationships and connect on a deeper level

Bulleted text
fails to capture
audience
attention

Missed opportunity
to make information
visual, digestible,
and memorable

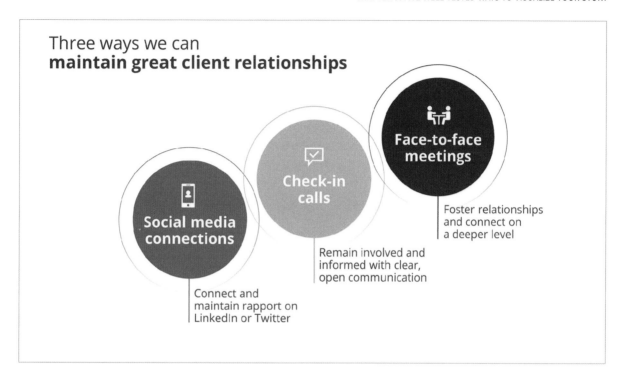

AFTER *What's working?*

Title is a headline (specifically identifies "three ways")

Colored shapes and icons help "chunk out" information, making content easy to understand

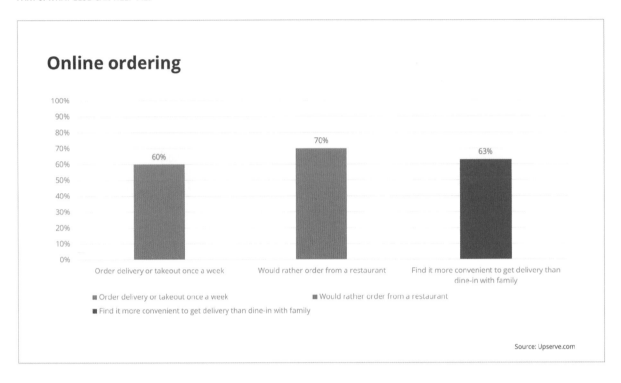

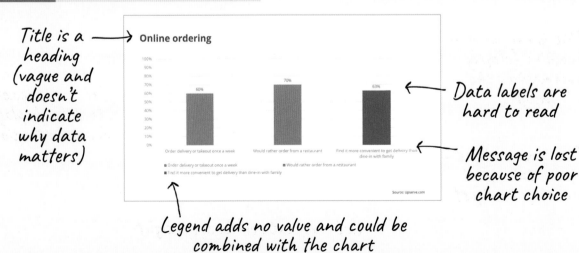

Savvy restaurateurs know the POWER of online ordering

60%
of U.S. consumers
order delivery or
takeout once a week

70%
Would rather
order directly
from a restaurant

63%
Find it more convenient
to get delivery than
dine-in with family

*Boost your bottom line with
an integrated ordering solution*

Source: Upserve.com

AFTER — *What's working?*

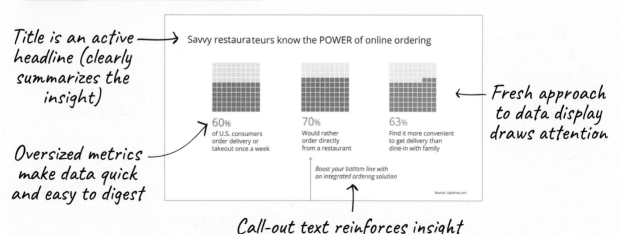

*Title is an active
headline (clearly
summarizes the
insight)*

*Oversized metrics
make data quick
and easy to digest*

*Fresh approach
to data display
draws attention*

Call-out text reinforces insight

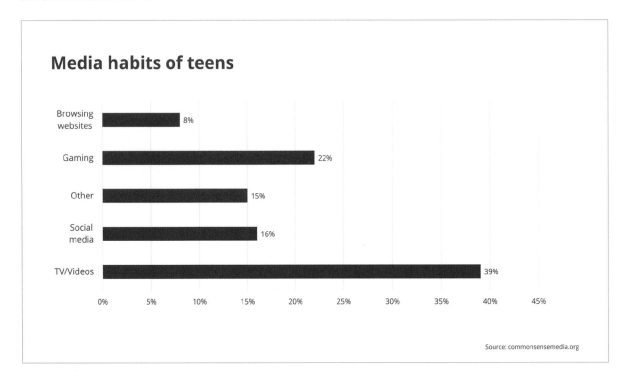

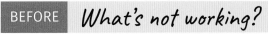 **BEFORE** *What's not working?*

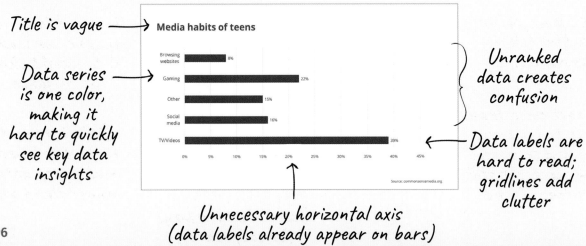

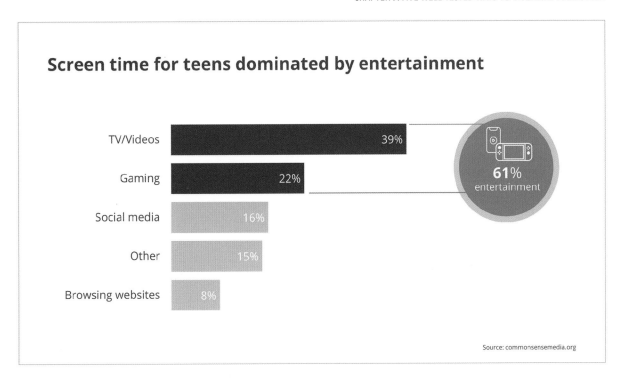

Screen time for teens dominated by entertainment

TV/Videos	39%
Gaming	22%
Social media	16%
Other	15%
Browsing websites	8%

61% entertainment

Source: commonsensemedia.org

AFTER *What's working?*

Title is an active headline (clearly summarizes key insight)

Contrast color draws focus to key data; grey used to subdue other data but still provides context

Oversized text with relevant icon makes data insight clear at-a-glance

Data is ranked highest to lowest making top data points stand out

Data labels are large for easy reading

Screen time for teens dominated by entertainment

TV/Videos	39%
Gaming	22%
Social media	16%
Other	15%
Browsing websites	8%

61% entertainment

Source: commonsensemedia.org

Top grossing movie distributors

		Movies	Total Gross	Market Share
1	Walt Disney	571	$39,688,247,167	16.94%
2	Warner Bros.	802	$35,592,155,457	15.19%
3	Sony Pictures	728	$28,777,646,671	12.28%
4	Universal	511	$27,464,279,056	11.72%
5	20th Century Fox	519	$25,853,240,689	11.04%
6	Paramount Pictures	481	$24,231,319,306	10.34%
7	Lionsgate	415	$9,537,881,421	4.07%
8	New Line	207	$6,194,343,024	2.64%
9	Dreamworks SKG	77	$4,278,649,271	1.83%
10	Miramax	384	$3,835,978,908	1.64%

https://www.the-numbers.com/market/distributors

BEFORE *What's not working?*

Title is a heading (vague) →

Top grossing movie distributors

		Movies	Total Gross	Market Share
1	Walt Disney	571	$39,688,247,167	16.94%
2	Warner Bros.	802	$35,592,155,457	15.19%
3	Sony Pictures	728	$28,777,646,671	12.28%
4	Universal	511	$27,464,279,056	11.72%
5	20th Century Fox	519	$25,853,240,689	11.04%
6	Paramount Pictures	481	$24,231,319,306	10.34%
7	Lionsgate	415	$9,537,881,421	4.07%
8	New Line	207	$6,194,343,024	2.64%
9	Dreamworks SKG	77	$4,278,649,271	1.83%
10	Miramax	384	$3,835,978,908	1.64%

https://www.the-numbers.com/market/distributors

Not clear what the key takeaway from the data is (nothing stands out)

Lack of abbreviation makes values hard to compare quickly

Top 2 movie distributors hold a third of total market share

RANK	DISTRIBUTOR	MOVIES	TOTAL GROSS	MARKET SHARE	
1	Walt Disney	571	$39.7B	16.9%	**32**%
2	Warner Bros	802	$35.6B	15.2%	
3	Sony Pictures	728	$28.8B	12.3%	
4	Universal	511	$27.5B	11.7%	
5	20th Century Fox	519	$25.9B	11.0%	
6	Paramount Pictures	481	$24.2B	10.3%	
7	Lionsgate	415	$9.5B	4.1%	
8	New Line	207	$6.2B	2.6%	
9	Dreamworks SKG	77	$4.3B	1.8%	
10	Miramax	384	$3.8B	1.6%	

https://www.the-numbers.com/market/distributors

AFTER   *What's working?*

Title is an active headline (clearly summarizes key insight)

Oversized text makes data insight clear at-a-glance

Green outline shape and text color draws focus to key data

Data retained for context, but subdued in grey

Abbreviated values make for easy comparison

Recycling waste

- 75% of waste is recyclable
  - Glass   – Tires
  - Paper   – Textiles
  - Cardboard – Batteries
  - Metal   – Electronics
  - Plastic
- Recycling plastic saves twice as much energy as it takes to burn it

Source: rubicon.com

BEFORE *What's not working?*

Title is a heading (vague) →

Recycling waste

- 75% of waste is recyclable
  - Glass   – Tires
  - Paper   – Textiles
  - Cardboard – Batteries
  - Metal   – Electronics
  - Plastic
- Recycling plastic saves twice as much energy as it takes to burn it

Source: rubicon.com

← *Detailed list distracts from key message, losing impact*

Photo is randomly placed, feels "small" and unimportant

AFTER *What's working?*

Title is a headline (concise, specific, conversational) →

Oversized text inside a colored shape makes data easy to scan

Photo is full screen, creating an intentional "mood" to anchor key insight

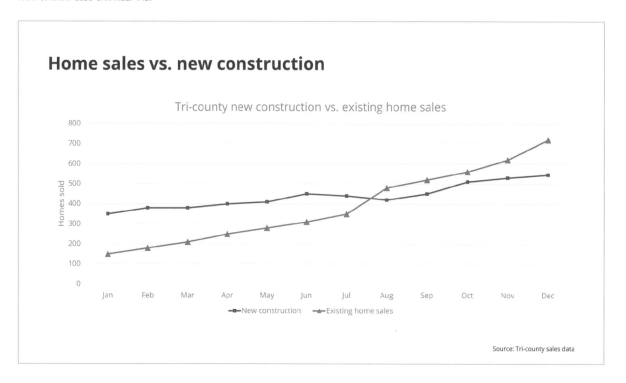

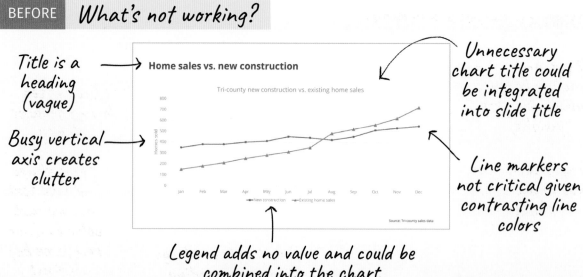

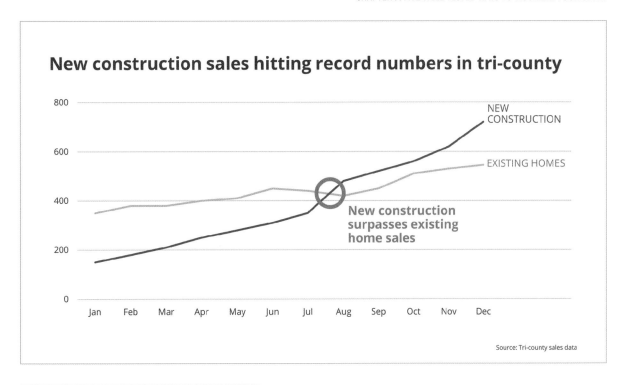

New construction sales hitting record numbers in tri-county

AFTER — *What's working?*

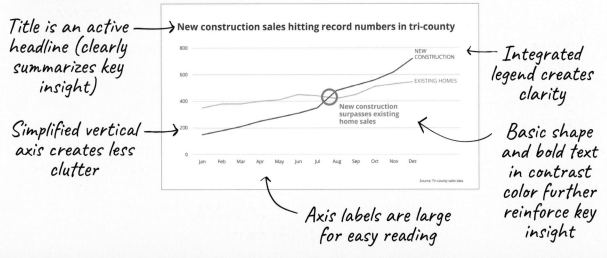

Title is an active headline (clearly summarizes key insight)

Simplified vertical axis creates less clutter

Axis labels are large for easy reading

Integrated legend creates clarity

Basic shape and bold text in contrast color further reinforce key insight

RECAP

Headlines, Your BIG Idea, and Intentional Visuals

You now have powerful tools in your toolkit—active headlines, a concise BIG Idea, and mindful visual techniques—that'll help your stories spring from their framework.

1

Headline news

The headline that blazes from the top of your slides (or one-pager, or email subject line) matters. Active headlines elevate your most consequential ideas above all the rest. They channel audience focus, help you control your narrative, and move your story forward.

2

What's your BIG Idea?

Your BIG Idea is a concise, specific, and conversational statement that encapsulates the WHAT of your story plus a few high-level benefits. It should offer crucial insight, be actionable, and focus entirely on the needs of your audience. Every fact, secondary idea, or piece of data should directly support your BIG Idea.

3

Five visualization techniques

Clever visuals are *always* strategic. Avoid the *Frankendeck* trap by patching together "pretty" slides from multiple sources with no clear narrative. Mindfully use simple, balanced, and not overly repetitive visuals to bring your story to life. Five well-tested visual techniques are photos, diagrams, data, text, and video.

PART 4

Let's see the magic!

How Does Storytelling Show Up in Everyday Business?

CHAPTER 10

Making a Recommendation

YOUR POCKETS ARE NOW FULL with a storytelling framework and process for how to map your ideas, facts, and data to it. You've been given power tools to fine-tune your narrative precision by learning to isolate your BIG Idea, use active headlines to push your story forward, and of course, light it all up with well-tested visualization techniques. You're now ready to see how all these ingredients are mixed together to create the magic.

We begin with one of the most common business scenarios that you, your boss, your co-workers, or basically anyone else doing business on this planet faces: making a recommendation.

Let's dig into two companies that are fictitious, yet face very common problems. For each scenario, you will see two different versions of the *same* set of recommendations—one good, one bad. We will guide you through both, calling out specifically what problems arise (all of them common) in the first version and what works well in the second version. And hopefully, given all you've learned in previous chapters, you will fully appreciate the difference. Off we go…

CASE STUDY

Urgent care... urgent problems

Harmony Health is a Seattle-based healthcare company with a network of hospitals, urgent cares, physicians, pharmacies, clinics, and laboratory services. Over the course of 60 years, they have expanded to three West Coast states, employing 8,500 people, with a network of 1,500 doctors in virtually every medical specialty.

Sensing an opportunity with younger Americans who frequent walk-in medical services, Harmony is currently developing a growth plan to build out their urgent care network. But they've got plenty of competition. There's an ever-growing crop of newer, retail-model urgent care centers (e.g., QuickCare, SpeedHealth, Dr. Zoom, etc.) that are also eager to expand.

And Harmony is facing another, potentially more serious, problem. Their urgent care patients are not happy with them. Reviews from popular consumer review sites are increasingly negative. The leadership team is so concerned with these reviews, they ran post-visit surveys to investigate further. To their dismay, many patients responded that they would not be returning to the clinic or recommending it to others.

A small, multi-departmental team, led by Customer Experience Strategy Director Theresa Nielsen, is on the case. She will convey to Harmony's leadership team why urgent care patients are unhappy and—before they consider increasing the number of clinics—recommend how they can address these problems.

BEFORE STORY | *What's not working?*

01

02

Update

- We need to make improvements both in the short term (via "quick wins") and long terms to establish a five star experience
- Technology needs to play a key role to help us imagine a best-in-class experience driven by innovation
- We need to involve the community by building relationships to improve access
- Online ratings for Harmony UC are low relative to our competition
- Reviews are negative with many reviewers mentioning our "dirty," "cluttered" and "messy" waiting rooms as key factor in why they don't return
- Observational field research (i.e., visits to our facilities) confirm these comments

03
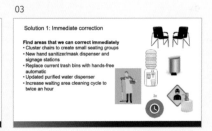

Resolution & Conflict

07

08

09
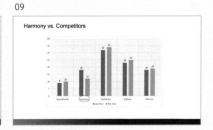

Setting & Characters

Welcome to an information dumping ground

And here it is... a troubled story that's not helping to sell its recommendations. Let's take a look under the hood and see what went wrong. The first problem emerges instantly: the story *begins* with recommendations (the resolution) before the audience learns WHY they should care about them. Conflict, which the resolution is solving, appears early on, but it's buried. When it appears again at the end of the story, it's too late. This story feels like a solution without a problem.

✗ **Conflict is buried**   ✗ **Headlines not active**   ✗ **Clunky visuals don't add value**

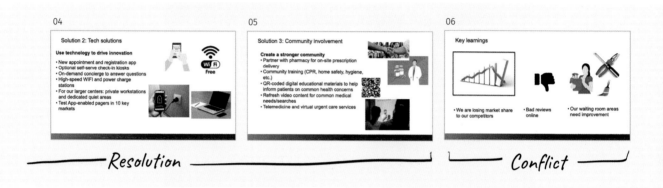

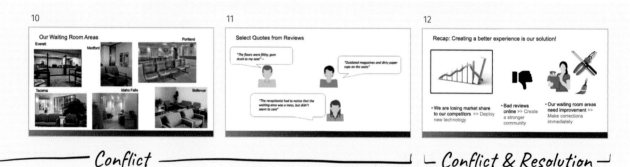

Setting and characters are buried as well. They come too late to set up the contextual meaning of the story. The narrative also lacks a BIG Idea that spells out WHAT the story is about and WHAT decision-makers should do. Vague, inactive slide titles don't move the story forward. And finally, the visuals are amateurish, lack a strategy, and don't enhance the story. Our analysis? This is more of a thought dumping ground than a real story.

BEFORE STORY *What's not working?*

01

Urgent Care Plan

Theresa Nielsen
Customer Experience Strategy Director

HarmonyHealth
Compassionate care for all

Title is bland and a missed opportunity to be active/ prescriptive

Title is a vague heading

02

Update

Presentation begins with resolution

- We need to make improvements both in the short term (via "quick wins") and long terms to establish a five star experience
- Technology needs to play a key role to help us imagine a best-in-class experience driven by innovation
- We need to involve the community by building relationships to improve access
- Online ratings for Harmony UC are low relative to our competition
- Reviews are negative with many reviewers mentioning our "dirty," "cluttered" and "messy" waiting rooms as key factor in why they don't return
- Observational field research (i.e., visits to our facilities) confirm these comments

Conflict is buried and doesn't adequately establish the WHY of this story

BEFORE STORY — *What's not working?*

03

Another vague title

Solution 1: Immediate correction

Find areas that we can correct immediately
- Cluster chairs to create small seating groups
- New hand sanitizer/mask dispenser and signage stations
- Replace current trash bins with hands-free automatic
- Updated purified water dispenser
- Increase waiting area cleaning cycle to twice an hour

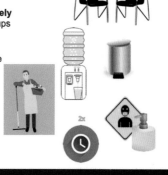

Clunky, randomly placed visual choices don't elevate the story

The HOW (resolution) details are revealed before audience knows WHY they should care

---

04

Vague, stagnant, title is a missed opportunity to advance the story

Solution 2: Tech solutions

Use technology to drive innovation
- New appointment and registration app
- Optional self-serve check-in kiosks
- On-demand concierge to answer questions
- High-speed WIFI and power charge stations
- For our larger centers: private workstations and dedicated quiet areas
- Test App-enabled pagers in 10 key markets

Distracting visuals are inconsistent in style and placement— they don't add value

The resolution bullets keep coming, it's still too early to be relevant

BEFORE STORY *What's not working?*

05

Solution 3: Community involvement

Create a stronger community
- Partner with pharmacy for on-site prescription delivery
- Community training (CPR, home safety, hygiene, etc.)
- QR-coded digital educational materials to help inform patients on common health concerns
- Refresh video content for common medical needs/searches
- Telemedicine and virtual urgent care services

Title is a vague heading

Visuals are meaningless because they're not mapped to ideas

More resolution without ever establishing context, again, why should anyone care?

06

Key learnings

- We are losing market share to our competitors
- Bad reviews online
- Our waiting room areas need improvement

This conflict slide needs a headline that signals the conflict

Visuals downgrade quality of the message

This slide spells out the conflict but comes far too late to make an impact

What's not working?

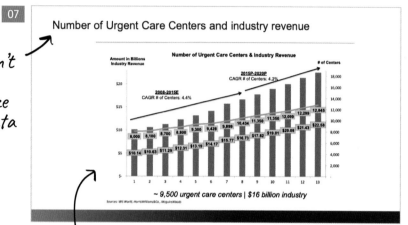

07

Title doesn't clearly summarize the key data insight

Chart offers a setting for the story but the information arrives too late to have value

08

Data is valuable to establish setting and characters but has lost its value so late in the story

Complicated chart is difficult to decipher— it relies heavily on the presenter to unpack

BEFORE STORY | *What's not working?*

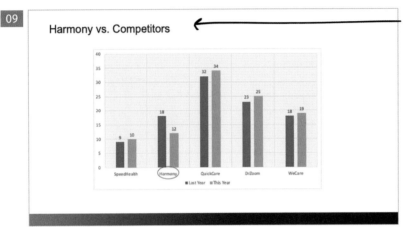

Ambiguous title doesn't tell audience what they need to know at a glance

Competitors = conflict but this is introduced far too late and its value is lost

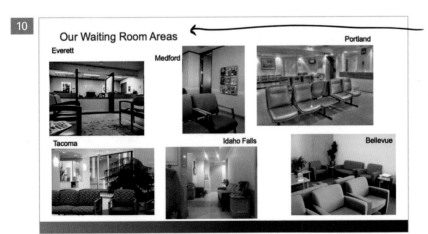

Title halts the story and offers no relevant insight

Visuals are uneven, hard to see, and don't add anything to narrative

BEFORE STORY *What's not working?*

Missed opportunity to connect the tone of these reviews and broadcast the real news

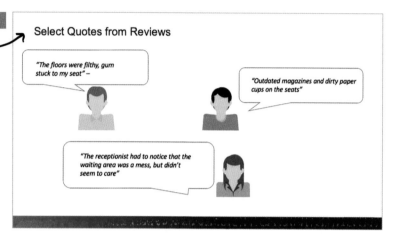

Select Quotes from Reviews

"The floors were filthy, gum stuck to my seat" –

"Outdated magazines and dirty paper cups on the seats"

"The receptionist had to notice that the waiting area was a mess, but didn't seem to care"

Three bad reviews spell conflict but this powerful message comes much too late

Title contains a BIG Idea (good) but it should have been introduced much earlier

Recap: Creating a better experience is our solution!

- We are losing market share to our competitors >> Deploy new technology
- Bad reviews online >> Create a stronger community
- Our waiting room areas need improvement >> Make corrections immediately

Visuals downgrade quality of the message

Good business stories shouldn't end with more conflict, they should always end with a BIG Idea

AFTER STORY — *What's working?*

01

02

03
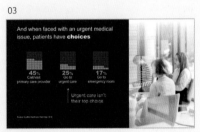

Setting & Characters

07

08
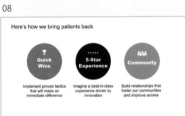

09

BIG Idea

Resolution

Get ready for the relief of a coherent story

Phew! What a difference a *real* story strategy makes. The same recommendations are reconfigured and redesigned in a narrative that flows through all four signposts *in the correct* order. Behold the crystal clear WHY, WHAT, and HOW that opens with a setting, characters, and then conflict. More conflict escalates the tension but is eased by the resolution landing page that previews each recommended path. (For more about landing pages, see *Chapter 18: Team Presentations: Who Does What?*)

✓ **Story has a clear WHY**   ✓ **Headlines are active**   ✓ **Simple visuals build mood**

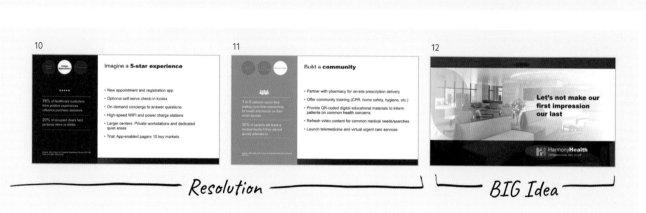

Another amazing transformation? A powerful BIG Idea introduced early and repeated in a soundbite at the end. This WHAT statement (plus one benefit) tells stakeholders what they need to know and do. Active headlines build on one another—especially the escalating conflict—and usher in the resolution. And subtle photos bring the story to life through every signpost, offering a consistent mood.

AFTER STORY *What's working?*

01

Active, information-rich title kicks off the story

02

Title is an active headline that clearly summarizes a key insight

This background photo sets the mood and doesn't distract from the data

The story opens with setting and characters to build context

AFTER STORY — *What's working?*

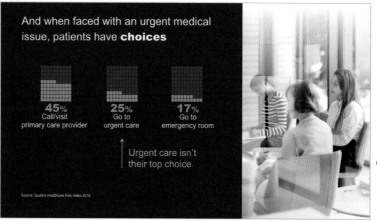

This headline builds on the one before it, advancing the story

Conflict introduced in yellow callout

Simple photos continue to set tone, illustrating the "characters" of this story

Setting and characters are further established with succinct data points (oversized and easy to scan)

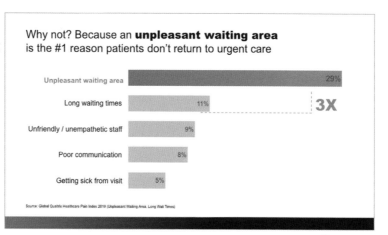

This active headline captures the powerful conflict and its key data point

Conflict is steadily building here ↗

AFTER STORY *What's working?*

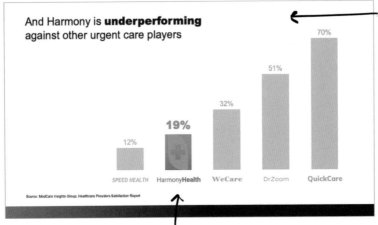

05

And Harmony is **underperforming** against other urgent care players

Conflict building continues and is well-captured in the headline

Harmony's performance is framed and called out perfectly here with color and enlarged metrics

06

To make matters worse, we're seeing an increasing amount of **negative customer feedback**

Transitional, active language like "to make matters worse" escalates the conflict

Text-heavy reviews are handled well visually, with plenty of spacing (and subtle photography)

AFTER STORY *What's working?*

⤷The BIG Idea lands right on time with a WHAT/BENEFIT statement that points directly at what the audience needs to know and do

The headline for the HOW of this story is explicit

Landing page shows a preview of three recommendations to resolve the conflict (placed in three distinct "buckets")

AFTER STORY *What's working?*

09

Implement quick wins

- Cluster chairs to create small seating groups
- Deploy new hand sanitizer/mask dispenser and signage stations
- Replace current trash bins with hands-free automatic
- Provide updated purified water dispenser
- Increase waiting area cleaning cycle to twice an hour

32% say they will walk away from a brand they love after just one bad experience

Though average wait time in urgent care nationwide is 21 minutes, patients are willing to wait longer in a more pleasant environment

Source: PwC Future of Customer Experience Survey 2017/18; UCAOA report, Patient Pop

Breadcrumb approach tells the audience— and the storyteller— exactly where the story is and where it is going

Data is used reservedly here, calling back to the conflict and upping the stakes for finding a good resolution

10

Imagine a 5-star experience

- New appointment and registration app
- Optional self-serve check-in kiosks
- On-demand concierge to answer questions
- High-speed WIFI and power charge stations
- Larger centers: Private workstations and dedicated quiet areas
- Trial: App-enabled pagers 10 key markets

78% of healthcare customers think positive experiences influence purchase decisions

20% of occupied chairs held personal items or drinks

Source: PwC Future of Customer Experience Survey 2017/18; Care Innovation Resources

Bullets are fine to list details, generally no more than 6 are recommended

Breadcrumbs continue to keep pace with the story and remind the audience where they are

What's working?

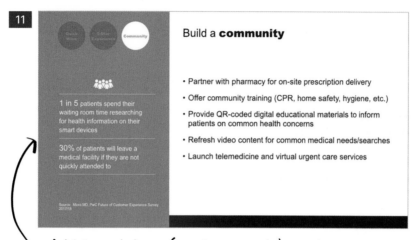

Additional data (used sparingly) continues to offer more fuel for each resolution

BIG Idea is powerfully repeated in a simple, easy-to-remember soundbite

THERE'S NOTHING LIKE A **POORLY CONCEIVED STORY** TO REMIND YOU WHAT A *RELIEF* A WELL-CONCEIVED ONE IS

CASE STUDY

Help wanted: Pilots

Miami-based Quantum Airlines has been operating worldwide for 25 years. Currently, the airline has nearly 13,500 employees with a fleet size of 196. Quantum serves 238 routes and 85 destinations. Despite the ups and downs of the airline industry, the company intends to expand over the next decade to meet expected passenger growth. Quantum's leaders seek to increase both its number of routes and the destinations it serves. They are particularly interested in an investment in the rapidly growing Asian market.

But the airline is also eyeing a risk factor that prevails across the entire airline industry—a pilot shortage. Like many of their competitors, they are concerned about finding and hiring qualified pilots to enable them to reach their growth goals. To mitigate this risk, the airline's leadership team has asked for some recommendations that will improve the way they identify and hire new talent.

Marco Vasquez, VP of People, must deliver three recommendations for the Quantum leadership team to approach the pilot shortage problem from various angles. This is how his original presentation turned out...

BEFORE STORY *What's not working?*

01

02

03

Resolution

07

08

09
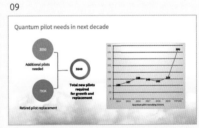

Setting & Characters

This story suffers from more than a pilot shortage

And boom. This story immediately starts with a resolution. Similar to the Harmony Health "before" story, no context is established and thus there is no WHY. Conflict comes later in the story, but it's never clear that it's an outside problem—the global pilot shortage. Characters and setting come nearly at the end—after the resolution—so this eliminated the relevance of this information. Marco included the four signposts, but in the wrong order. *No credit Marco.*

✗ WHY comes too late	✗ Headlines missing key insight	✗ Data overload obscures key points

04

05

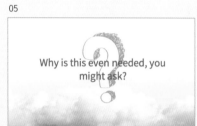

06

Resolution — *Setting & Characters* —

10

11

Resolution —

BEFORE STORY *What's not working?*

01 Future Growth Planning

QUANTUM AIRLINES

Marco Vasquez
VP of People

Photo has nothing to do with airline industry (other than the clouds)

02

1 Candidate Outreach Efforts

- Develop mentorship program to ensure that newly hired pilots are ready to work and fly with Quantum
- Implement new screening and selection process which we will develop in the next 6-12 months
- Groom future potential captains through training and mentorship
- Launch new training that is adaptive, data-driven and customized
- Implement new competency gap and pilot performance assessment

Headline lacks any real news, it just serves as a label for the list

Information is dumped in bulleted text and hard to scan

Story starts with resolution, before context is established, offering no reason to care

BEFORE STORY *What's not working?*

03

2 Targeting Female Pilots

- Today, women account for approximately 5.4% of airline commercial pilots globally
- Increase the number of female pilots we hire
- Create more female-friendly schedule, culture and working policies
- Develop outreach and flight training sponsorship program
- Role model and engage girls through STEM program early

Vague heading misses opportunity to broadcast real insights

Data is relevant but doesn't sync well with other resolution points

---

04

3 Attracting future candidates

- Partner with CAE, major aviation colleges and universities to develop flight academy program and curricula to attract future candidates
- Subsidize or sponsor recruits who are high-potential
- Partner with banks to provide financing options and low-interest aviation student loans
- Implement new compensation and signing bonus model as further incentive
- Launch pre-hire onboarding program so they get up-to-speed quickly

180K pilots must transition to captains in next decade

This is good (but misplaced) data that would work better for conflict escalation

The story continues to list resolution details and yet, no clear WHY has been established

BEFORE STORY *What's not working?*

05

Why is this even needed, you might ask?

Here's a setup to the WHY (finally) but it belongs much earlier in the story

06

Rationale for our recommendation

GROWTH

- Passenger numbers are forecast to double from 2010 to 2030; i.e., 3.5% CAGR
- In 2000, the average citizen flew just once every 43 months. In 2017, the figure was once every 22 months
- Growth will come from Asia (see next slide)

US +59%

China +167%

India +262%

Thailand +118%

Indonesia +219%

Rationale for an upcoming solution is good, but it should come before the resolution

Data establishes context through setting and characters but relevance is lost when it comes this late

| BEFORE STORY | *What's not working?* |

07

Rationale continues but, again, it should precede the resolution (not follow it)

Rationale for our recommendation

PILOT COMPOSITION
- 50% of pilots flying by 2027 have not yet started to train
- In the U.S., women account for 12% of pilot students, showing a strong upward trend
- From 2003 to 2016, 35% fewer students completed academic programs for airline/commercial/professional pilot and flight crew
- To complete a commercial aviation program and flight hours to qualify costs $125K on average

Data points are all associated with different recommendations, so the narrative flow is lost

08

Headline includes a potential conflict but without tension-building language it falls flat

Number of new pilots needed in next decade

150K
Active pilot pool to meet demand

255K
Total new pilot required for growth and replacement

105K
Retired pilot replacement

10-year Pilot demand by region

AMERICAS +85K New pilots

EUROPE +50K New pilots

MIDDLE EAST & AFRICA +30K New pilots

ASIA-PACIFIC +90K New pilots

Too much ancillary data causes key points to get lost

What's not working?

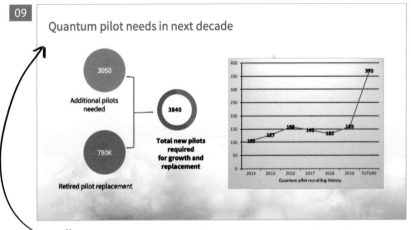

Graph is poorly labeled and hard to read, the value is lost

"Pilot needs" are a heading, not a headline—what are the pilot needs? The headline should offer a solid takeaway

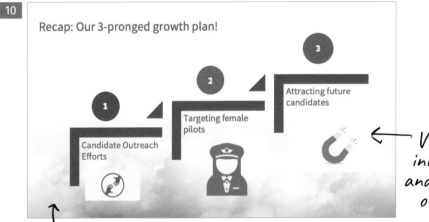

Visuals are inconsistent and overshadowing text

Resolution recap language is confusing because it's not consistent with prior language

BEFORE STORY *What's not working?*

A more airline-relevant photo would better show off theme and mood →

Generic call to action is a missed opportunity to recap a true BIG Idea

AFTER STORY *What's working?*

01

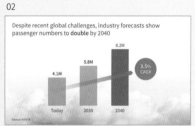

02

Despite recent global challenges, industry forecasts show passenger numbers to **double** by 2040

03

Growth will come primarily from Asia, with India showing the highest percentage increase in new passengers

Setting & Characters

07

Our plan for winning critical new talent

08

Find the right stuff

09

Grow the next gen

Resolution

Get signposts in order and let the magic happen

Ahhhh... The relief of a well-told story. Marco got this version *very* right with each signpost revealed in the correct order. He sets the market scene and establishes characters early: despite some recent bumps in the road, industry forecasts show passenger numbers to double in ten years, with growth coming primarily from Asia. He then introduces the obvious conflict—a global pilot shortage—and finally closes the resolution—a talent acquisition plan that will ensure Quantum isn't left

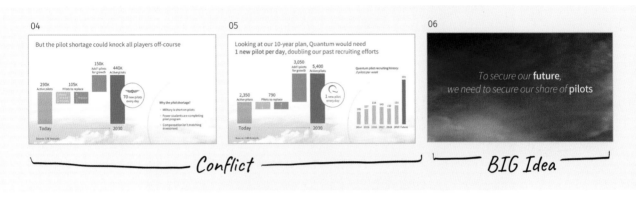

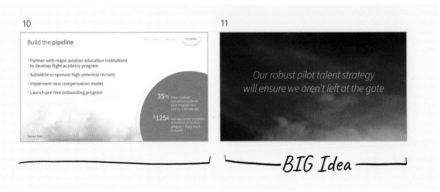

behind. Notice how the story signposts are bolstered and visually called out with carefully selected data. Critical to note: data *supports* his story but it never overtakes or obscures the plot.

Every headline is active in this story, driving the narrative forward—particularly the conflict. Marco hits hard with his BIG Idea (restated in a soundbite form at the end) and uses a landing page to preview his three resolutions. Each resolution is placed in a clean bucket, and they are then repeated as visual "breadcrumbs" to guide the narrative flow. Marco ties it all together with his cloudy, mood-setting, elegant photography. *A+ Marco!*

AFTER STORY · *What's working?*

← *Photo is subtle, appropriate, and sets the mood*

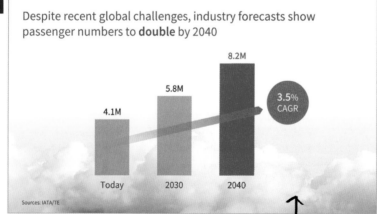

← *Active headline immediately establishes setting with steep market growth rate*

Growth rate clearly called out and is well-corelated with the headline

AFTER STORY | *What's working?*

Headline introduces characters (passengers) and advances the story

03

Growth will come primarily from Asia, with India showing the highest percentage increase in new passengers

Select data callouts support the headline

"But" is a great way to introduce conflict

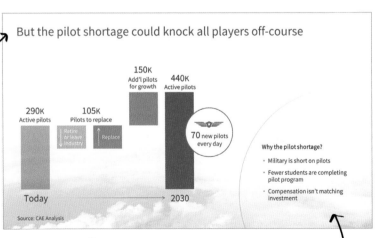

04

But the pilot shortage could knock all players off-course

Secondary data provides more backstory but doesn't steal the show

AFTER STORY *What's working?*

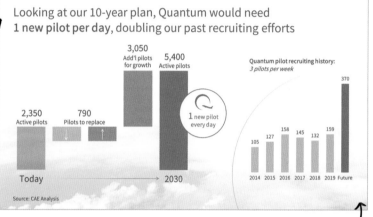

Conflict escalates with this headline

Data supports conflict and tension showing clearly that past recruiting efforts will not support future needs

BIG Idea arrives to ease some tension, showing the audience they will see a brighter future

AFTER STORY *What's working?*

A simple landing page previews three paths to resolve the conflict →

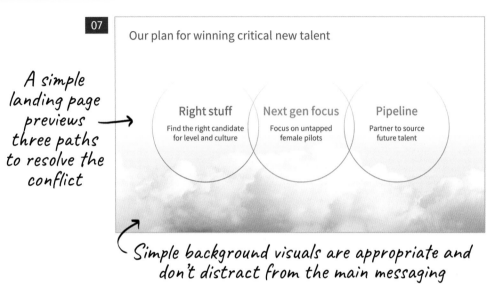

Simple background visuals are appropriate and don't distract from the main messaging

Headline is active and well-connected to the resolution

Bread-crumbs show where the story is and where it is going

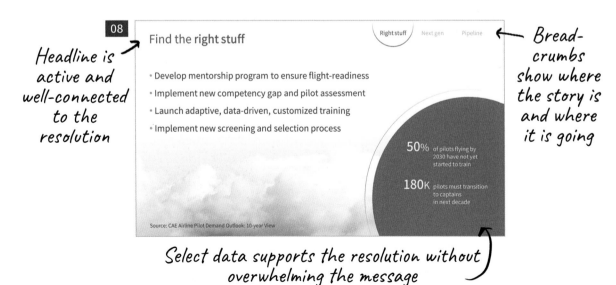

Select data supports the resolution without overwhelming the message

141

AFTER STORY *What's working?*

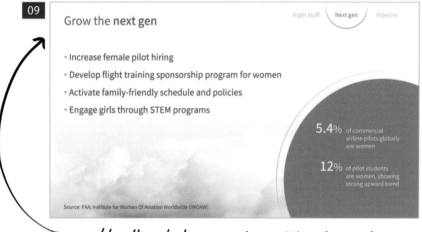

Subtle breadcrumbs continue to trace the path of the story

Headline helps easy transition to next recommendation

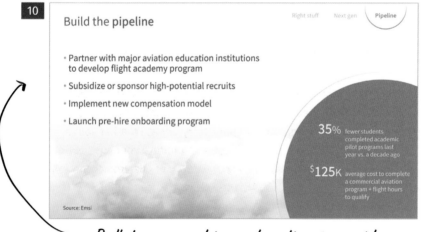

A couple of data points provide additional background to support the resolution

Bullets are used in moderation to avoid oversaturation of information

AFTER STORY *What's working?*

Our robust pilot talent strategy will ensure we aren't left at the gate

The BIG Idea restated in a soundbite reiterates the need to update the recruitment strategy

IN SHORT...

Give your recommendations their best chance

Two common business scenarios. Two stark examples of the difference between recommendations that can either be elevated through good storytelling or diminished through poor storytelling. Whether you're making a case to hire more talent, hoping to improve your customers' experience, or looking to resolve any other type of business challenge, wouldn't you rather give your ideas their best chance to influence decision-makers?

We bet you would (just make sure to have a clear WHY, WHAT, and HOW).

CHAPTER 11

Providing an Update

"HEY, HOW'S YOUR PROJECT GOING?"

Everybody at some point has been asked to show the status of a program or project. And many of us simply default to using an existing template and revise it each month or quarter. Pretty straightforward, right? Unfortunately, not so much. As the weeks and months go on, these templates have a tendency to morph and flex to encompass the growing feedback of various stakeholders. What starts off as a simple update will eventually feel like you're trying to tame a wild beast.

Surely, this isn't a time to bring in storytelling to communicate the most routine, unsexy update, right?

Nope. Absolutely wrong.

Updates are a great opportunity to strategically insert a story structure and demonstrate you're able to communicate the health of the project inside and out. But be aware, when communicating an update, your status report will likely fall into one of two "camps." It will either come *with* a conflict or *without* a conflict. Each type of update has its own important distinctions. Let's take a closer look.

When your update has <u>conflict</u>

When your update has conflict, it's time to roll out your full baseline story structure. Begin with setting and characters to report what's been accomplished in your project or program since your last check-in. Then move into your conflict by identifying a challenge (or challenges) that are impacting (or might impact) the project or

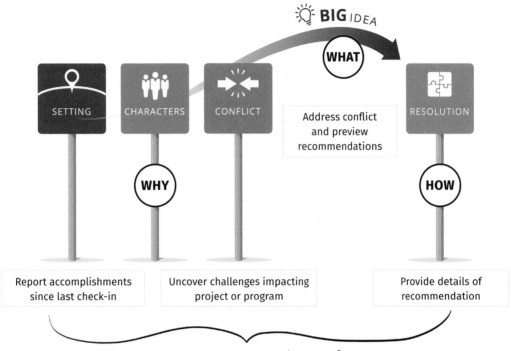

For updates with conflict, apply the baseline story structure

program—it could be delays, budget shortfalls, resource constraints, scope change, or new competition. Next, bring in your BIG Idea to directly address the conflict. Preview your recommendation and then lay out the details of your resolution. And there's your story. This is similar to *Chapter 10: Making a Recommendation*.

When your update has no conflict

But what if your project is going just fine and there is no conflict? Well, first, congratulations! If there are truly no present (or future) concerns, you only need some of the story elements. Just establish setting and characters to convey what your team has accomplished in your project or program. The main goal is to show that everything is progressing on time and on budget. You might even dig out your original recommendation or proposal and compare your characters' situation today to how things were at the outset. Your BIG Idea is a simple soundbite that basically says, "we're on track" (it contains a WHAT statement only and no benefit). And since there is no conflict, no resolution is necessary—the BIG Idea will suffice on its own. Keep in mind: updates without conflict are tactical. *You might not even need to hold an actual meeting.* Perhaps you can convey that the project is on track in an email or through a project management tool. After all, it never hurts to spare everyone another meeting!

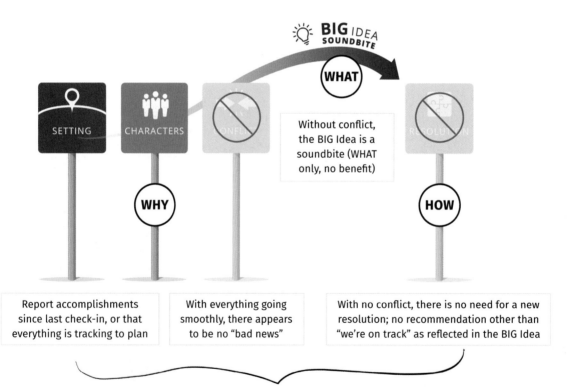

For updates without conflict, only a few of the baseline story structure elements apply

CONFLICT-LESS UPDATES
ARE TACTICAL

SAVE YOUR AUDIENCE (AND YOURSELF)
FROM A MEETING AND SIMPLY PROVIDE
A STATUS UPDATE OFFLINE

But wait. You're *sure* there's no conflict?

We don't want to make anyone paranoid, but where you don't see conflict, there might be conflict. Do you truly want to offer a tactical update? (Because without conflict, that's what it is.) Or do you want to take this opportunity to be more strategic? If you do, then by all means *dig dig dig* to discover any possible concerns that'll elevate your strategic role on this project. And to make your digging easier, here are three ways to discover conflict in your update: lean on yourself, lean on a trusted colleague, or lean on your audience. (Stay with us here.)

Start by seeking to broaden *your* individual scope. Are there any new angles, insights, or opportunities you can provide? Conversely, are there any potential pitfalls or risks that might lay ahead?

Secondly, talk to a (smart) colleague who's had different experiences than you (bonus if they are familiar with your project or worked on a similar one in the past) and might detect a missed conflict. They might also point out broader opportunities to embrace.

Finally, you can open up your search for conflict to your audience. Yes, you read that correctly. After you share your setting and characters, open up the dialogue to your audience and glean their opinion about anything that could be a "red flag." Now, granted, this can be pretty risky—and you better do your homework first— but fielding audience engagement brings shared ownership. Your audience will appreciate your open curiosity about any potential risk to the project. If actual conflict emerges through this dialogue, be ready to take note of this new wrinkle and circle back to it—with your resolution—in your next update.

Let's now take a look at how to build an update with conflict using a real (actually, fictitious) story.

CASE STUDY

Strong sales. Implementation? Not so much.

LearnForward is an educational technology company that provides software as a service (SaaS) to colleges and universities, K–12 schools, government agencies, nonprofits, and businesses of all shapes and sizes. Over ten million students, faculty, employers, and government entities at 1,300 institutions rely on the platform. LearnForward's sales numbers are robust with a growing network of academic institutions, government agencies, and businesses.

But what isn't reflected in the sales numbers is that in Q1, software implementations for the majority of LearnForward's new customers were slow. Only half as many went live as were projected in the previous quarter. And the data shows exactly where and why the problem is happening. Most customers who remain in the technical set-up phase too long were international clients—especially those in Australia and New Zealand. Some clients were stalled in implementation because they require more data security, others wanted extra features, and still others were affected by changing market conditions. Implementation Program Manager Hanae Tanaka has been asked to update the executive team. While the sales performance looks like great news, she must also alert them to the serious implementation problems and offer recommendations to speed up the process.

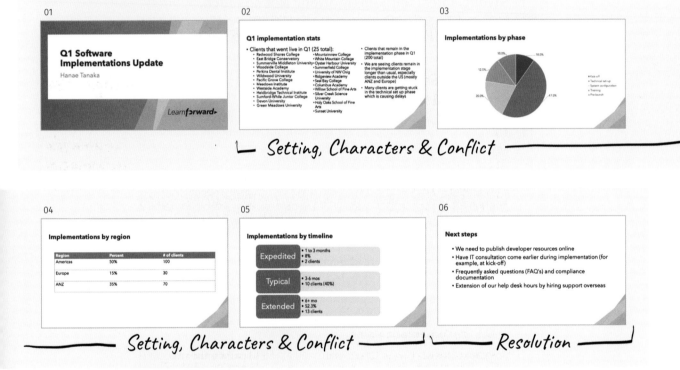

BEFORE STORY — *What's not working?*

Setting, Characters & Conflict

Setting, Characters & Conflict — **Resolution**

The lead is buried deep… very deep

This LearnForward update seems like a routine, conflict-free report, but upon closer look, the data reveals something very different. A glaring conflict is visible (if you stare long enough): 50% of all new client implementations are stalled. Unfortunately, this news is buried in both walls of text and confusing charts. More data reveals the problem by phase, region, and timeline. And yet, every opportunity to call out this conflict is missed both in charts and in each of the headlines. There is an old expression: *don't point to the spot on the rug.* It doesn't apply here. Point to the spot and never bury conflict in an update.

| ✗ No BIG Idea | ✗ Passive headings | ✗ Conflict lost in data |

01

Q1 Software Implementations Update

Hanae Tanaka

Learn**f⊃rward**▸

← Vague title offers no hint that meaningful information is to come

02

Q1 implementation stats

- Clients that went live in Q1 (25 total):
  - Redwood Shores College
  - East Bridge Conservatory
  - Summerville Middleton University
  - Woodside College
  - Perkins Dental Institute
  - Wildwood University
  - Pacific Grove College
  - Meadows Institute
  - Westside Academy
  - Heldbridge Technical Institute
  - Sumford-While Junior College
  - Devon University
  - Green Meadows University
  - Mountainview College
  - White Mountain College
  - Oyster Harbour University
  - Summerfield College
  - University of NW Osig
  - Ridgeview Academy
  - Seal Bay College
  - Columbus Academy
  - Willow School of Fine Arts
  - Silver Creek Science University
  - Holy Oaks School of Fine Arts
  - Sunset University

- Clients that remain in the implementation phase in Q1 (200 total)

- We are seeing clients remain in the implementation stage longer than usual, especially clients outside the US (mostly ANZ and Europe)

- Many clients are getting stuck in the technical set up phase which is causing delays

It is unnecessary to jam every client on the slide

The important conflict is hinted at but deeply buried

BEFORE STORY *What's not working?*

03

This heading misses the important insight that half the clients are stalled in technical set up

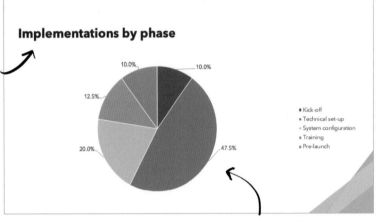

Implementations by phase

10.0%
10.0%
12.5%
20.0%
47.5%

- Kick-off
- Technical set-up
- System configuration
- Training
- Pre-launch

The pie chart reveals that 50% of new clients are parked in the set-up phase but it is not called out in any way

04

Implementations by region

Region	Percent	# of clients
Americas	50%	100
Europe	15%	30
ANZ	35%	70

This unclear chart forces viewer to figure out data on their own

Regional data offers more detail about where implementation problems are occurring (ANZ/Europe)

BEFORE STORY *What's not working?*

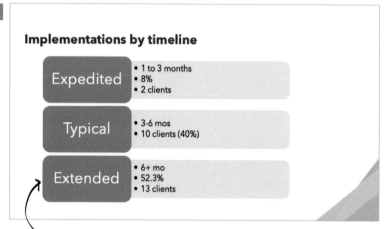

Implementations by timeline

Expedited
- 1 to 3 months
- 8%
- 2 clients

Typical
- 3-6 mos
- 10 clients (40%)

Extended
- 6+ mo
- 52.3%
- 13 clients

This chart again, fails to point out the key data insight: half the clients are lagging in "extended" implementation

Next steps

- We need to publish developer resources online
- Have IT consultation come earlier during implementation (for example, at kick-off)
- Frequently asked questions (FAQ's) and compliance documentation
- Extension of our help desk hours by hiring support overseas

Bullets are confusing because grammar is not consistent— some start with a verb, others a noun

This resolution slide is vague and doesn't clearly connect to the conflict

AFTER STORY *What's working?*

01

Q1 Update: A path towards faster implementations

Hanae Tanaka

Learn**f**ɔrward▸

02

In Q1, 25 clients went "live", launching their new LearnForward systems

25 Clients went live
Only half as many as projected

200 Clients remain in implementation
Up slightly from 185 in Q4 2019

Breakdown by phase, region and timeline has shifted

03

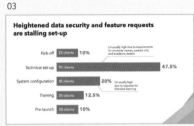

Heightened data security and feature requests are stalling set-up

— Setting & Characters →

Conflict

07

Our path to better enablement

Publish
developer resources online

Initiate
IT consultation earlier (at kick-off)

Build
IT guide including FAQ and compliance documentation

Extend
help desk hours by hiring support overseas

08

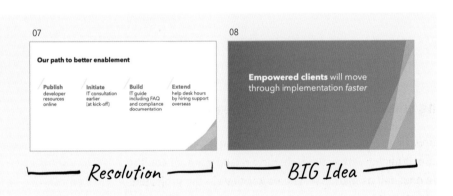

Empowered clients will move through implementation *faster*

Resolution

BIG Idea

154

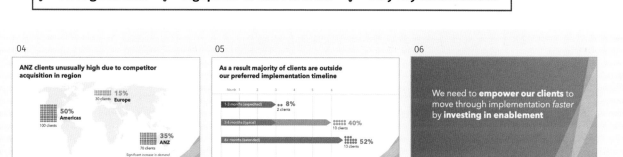

Identifying conflict and solving it makes you a hero

This LearnForward update gets it right by unleashing the full baseline story structure. It begins with setting, characters, and a hint of conflict right on slide one: half as many new clients went live in the projected timeframe *and* stalled implementations were getting worse. *(Uh oh.)* The conflict then escalates, showing WHY these installations are getting stalled: some clients are requiring more data security and extra features. Others are affected by changing market conditions.

Then the BIG Idea is introduced: *LearnForward must invest in better enablement.* The story dives into the resolution—divided neatly into four visual buckets—and then wraps up by revisiting the BIG Idea. This update is fast, useful, and very thorough. *A decision-maker's dream.*

AFTER STORY *What's working?*

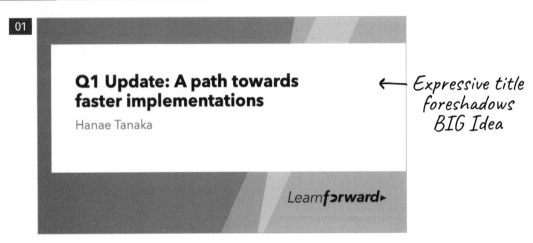

← *Expressive title foreshadows BIG Idea*

← *Headline quickly helps set the scene with setting and characters*

Data hints at conflict, teeing up the next signpost

AFTER STORY — *What's working?*

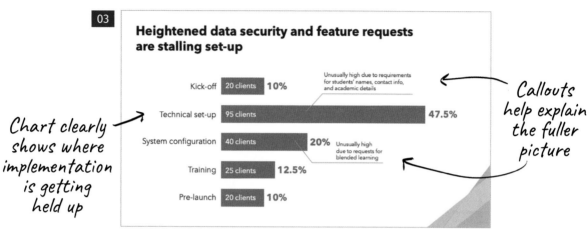

03

Heightened data security and feature requests are stalling set-up

Stage	Clients	%
Kick-off	20 clients	10%
Technical set-up	95 clients	47.5%
System configuration	40 clients	20%
Training	25 clients	12.5%
Pre-launch	20 clients	10%

Unusually high due to requirements for students' names, contact info, and academic details

Unusually high due to requests for blended learning

Chart clearly shows where implementation is getting held up

Callouts help explain the fuller picture

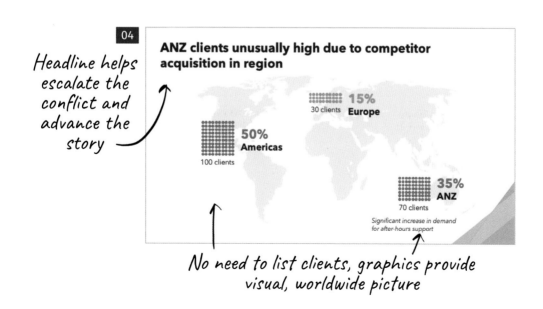

04

ANZ clients unusually high due to competitor acquisition in region

15% **Europe** — 30 clients

50% **Americas** — 100 clients

35% **ANZ** — 70 clients

Significant increase in demand for after-hours support

Headline helps escalate the conflict and advance the story

No need to list clients, graphics provide visual, worldwide picture

AFTER STORY *What's working?*

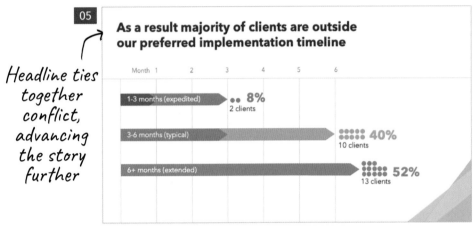

05

As a result majority of clients are outside our preferred implementation timeline

Month 1   2   3   4   5   6

1-3 months (expedited) •• **8%**
2 clients

3-6 months (typical) ::::: **40%**
10 clients

6+ months (extended) ::::: **52%**
13 clients

Headline ties together conflict, advancing the story further

Clean chart shows data that supports the headline

06

We need to **empower our clients** to move through implementation *faster* by **investing in enablement**

BIG Idea follows conflict with a benefit and WHAT statement

AFTER STORY *What's working?*

07

Our path to better enablement

Headline signals multiple paths to resolve implementation conflict

| **Publish** | **Initiate** | **Build** | **Extend** |
| developer resources online | IT consultation earlier (at kick-off) | IT guide including FAQ and compliance documentation | help desk hours by hiring support overseas |

Resolution placed in visual "buckets" that are easy to scan and digest

08

Empowered clients will move through implementation *faster*

BIG Idea repeats in a soundbite variation

BE AN
Update Hero

Don't shy away from conflict

Like recommendations, updates that include conflict should take the audience through the WHY, WHAT, and HOW of a story, including all four signposts and a BIG Idea. Conflict-free updates should scale down to include just the first two signposts, setting and characters, and offer a simple performance measurement. But make no mistake: few projects, product launches, consulting assignments, etc. go *perfectly* smoothly. If you want to drive up your value on the project—and your career—think strategically. Look hard for any problems lurking around the corner and always strive to pinpoint new opportunities.

Don't just check the box—be an update hero.

CHAPTER 12

Crafting an Email

WE'VE ALL BEEN IGNORED. Every single one of us has carefully worded a high-stakes email that's been met with... *crickets*. And it's no wonder. The average full-time worker gets 120 emails per day and spends nearly *one-third* of their day (and who are we kidding, probably part of their night) reading and answering email.[1] For executives, who are basically nonstop decision-machines, *it's a whole lot more*. We've spent years examining how to grab the attention of these busy decision-makers, and one thing is absolutely clear: if you can't cut through the noise, you don't have a chance of being heard.

Amazingly, for such an integral part of how we do business, sending a compelling email is *rarely* taught. So, let's teach you how to cut through the noise, which—you guessed it—comes down to business storytelling.

Every email is an opportunity to tell a story

We work with some of the biggest, fastest-paced brands in the world. We—like everyone else—have been occasionally left in the dark with ignored emails. It doesn't feel great. We've also *received* thousands of emails that leave us confused, overwhelmed, even annoyed. Clearly, there is a lot of wasted email energy going around! We grew so curious about this, we started to seriously observe our own interaction with clients and partners to uncover which content got a quick response and which content, ah... *languished*.

We saw two things immediately: First, standards for communications are sky-high. In other words, expectations are that every high-stakes email is thorough, strategic, and designed for action. No slap-dashed, unpunctuated, half-sentences. (Perhaps you think this makes you *look* busy but, in fact, it throws extra question on the validity of your ideas.) Second, emails that get answered are lean and cut through the noise, but (and this is a big but), they aren't necessarily *super*-short. We've observed that *more* information in the right order and degree of detail is better than a few abbreviated lines (you never want to raise more questions than you answer!).

Not every email needs to be a perfect story, but it is very clear that good emails exhibit the same baseline story structure (like any presentation or meeting), which includes an easily discernable WHY, WHAT, and HOW. Let's take a look at two versions of the same email from two companies you're familiar with, Harmony Health and Quantum Airlines. We first met these companies a few chapters back, so if you want more of their backstory, refer to *Chapter 10: Making a Recommendation.*

CASE STUDY

An email begging to be ignored

You might recall that Harmony Health has a network of urgent care clinics looking to expand into a crowded market. Unfortunately, they found through both post-appointment surveys and consumer website reviews that patients were unhappy with the ambiance of their facilities—particularly the waiting rooms. Theresa Nielsen, Customer Experience Strategy Director, is preparing for a meeting with her leadership team to address this problem. To gather crucial input for this meeting with the bosses, she is hoping to gather insights from her colleagues that'll help fuel her recommendations to improve the clinic waiting room experience. Here are two different versions of the same email.

BEFORE STORY *What's not working?*

Vague subject line is a missed opportunity to state BIG Idea

Meeting preparation

TN Theresa Nielsen <Theresa.nielsen@harmonyhealth.com>
To Customer Experience Team

↩ Reply   ↩ Reply All   → Forward   ⋯

Wednesday, March 20, 12:52 PM

Hi Team,

I'm preparing for a meeting next week and am looking for your input on "Quick Wins" section of the Urgent Care document.

I've included the link. Can you review this document and provide any helpful feedback as soon as possible? I want to make sure our document is comprehensive and on-point. I'll take your ideas and edit them down as needed.

Thanks to all of you for your feedback and inputs to our recommended fixes!

Best,

Theresa

Theresa Nielsen
Customer Experience Strategy Director

HarmonyHealth
Compassionate care for all

Meeting context is missing, leaving recipients wondering why they are receiving this email

Resolution is unclear with no specific details of the ask

✗ **No context established**   ✗ **Vague subject line**   ✗ **Resolution ask is unclear**

What you see here is a completely missed opportunity to tell a story. There is absolutely no clear WHY, WHAT, and HOW in this message. There are no signposts. There is no BIG Idea. While Theresa might have thought her short, succinct email would make it easier for her colleagues to read and understand what she was asking them to do, it actually made it harder and more confusing. Let's take a closer look.

First of all, the subject line is totally passive: *meeting preparation.* As this email lands at the top of the recipients' inbox, they can't tell *which* meeting the sender is referring to and who needs to do the preparation. This vague subject line offers no important information and is begging to be ignored. Since the subject line is an opportunity to introduce the BIG Idea of a story (telling the recipient exactly what you want them to know or do) this attempt is a big fail. Scanning this subject line, there will certainly be confusion among Theresa's colleagues about WHAT they are being asked to click on.

Let's move on to the body of the email where, unfortunately, all four signposts are missing in action. Let's start with the WHY, the context. This wording may leave the recipient wondering why they are receiving this email: *I'm preparing for a meeting next week and am looking for your input on "Quick Wins" section of the Urgent Care document.*

They might wonder, what upcoming meeting? Who's attending said meeting? What is the goal of the meeting? Many times, the context for an email was communicated verbally, but a follow-on email that does not go back and reestablish the context will always leave a lot of confusion. Theresa should have brought her colleagues up to date with a setting and characters.

And of course, Theresa is also missing conflict here. She does not actually spell out what problem they are trying to solve. She is assuming that every one of her recipients is bought into the urgency of the issue (if they can figure out what it is) and will want to put it in their "respond right away" folder.

And finally—crucially—there is no resolution. Nowhere are there any specific details of Theresa's ask. She is looking for feedback from her colleagues, but what kind? Without a stated conflict and BIG Idea, it is nearly impossible to understand what she is looking for. She also doesn't offer a deadline or a true call to action for this request, which is going to help ensure this short, sweet email starts gathering dust.

AFTER STORY *What's working?*

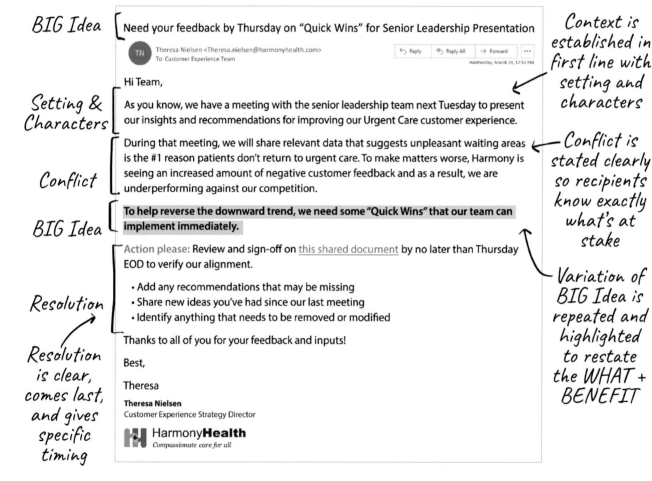

BIG Idea

Setting & Characters

Conflict

BIG Idea

Resolution

Resolution is clear, comes last, and gives specific timing

Context is established in first line with setting and characters

Conflict is stated clearly so recipients know exactly what's at stake

Variation of BIG Idea is repeated and highlighted to restate the WHAT + BENEFIT

Need your feedback by Thursday on "Quick Wins" for Senior Leadership Presentation

Theresa Nielsen <Theresa.nielsen@harmonyhealth.com>
To Customer Experience Team

↩ Reply   ↩ Reply All   → Forward   ⋯
Wednesday, March 20, 12:52 PM

Hi Team,

As you know, we have a meeting with the senior leadership team next Tuesday to present our insights and recommendations for improving our Urgent Care customer experience.

During that meeting, we will share relevant data that suggests unpleasant waiting areas is the #1 reason patients don't return to urgent care. To make matters worse, Harmony is seeing an increased amount of negative customer feedback and as a result, we are underperforming against our competition.

To help reverse the downward trend, we need some "Quick Wins" that our team can implement immediately.

Action please: **Review and sign-off on** this shared document by no later than Thursday EOD to verify our alignment.

- Add any recommendations that may be missing
- Share new ideas you've had since our last meeting
- Identify anything that needs to be removed or modified

Thanks to all of you for your feedback and inputs!

Best,

Theresa

Theresa Nielsen
Customer Experience Strategy Director

HarmonyHealth
Compassionate care for all

✓ **Subject line = BIG Idea** ✓ **Context comes first** ✓ **Conflict stated clearly**

At last... an email that tells a story

Behold, here is a new version of Theresa's email that tells a story and will more surely compel her colleagues to respond to her request. First, notice that—yes—this email is longer. And that's okay. An email *can* be longer if it provides meaningful context to the recipient.

The BIG Idea comes roaring out right in the subject line: *Need your feedback by Thursday on "Quick Wins" for Senior Leadership Presentation.*

Theresa's colleagues see immediately what she wants them to know and do. Getting this message right—so they fully understand what's at stake—in the subject line is the primary reason her email will be opened or ignored.

THE SUBJECT LINE IS YOUR FIRST POINT OF ENTRY INTO YOUR RECEIVER'S SPHERE OF ATTENTION—MAKE IT COUNT.

She then begins to establish context right in the opening line of the email through setting and characters. This completely cuts any confusion as to WHY the recipient is getting the email: *As you know, we have a meeting with the senior leadership team next Tuesday to present our insights and recommendations for improving our Urgent Care customer experience.*

Her colleagues know they are receiving the email because they are participating in a meeting next week. She also brings in three characters to her story: the reader, the leadership team, and of course, herself. What is the setting? Well, the urgent care centers for one, but more immediately, the meeting everyone is going to be attending! In one line, the reader knows WHY this email is relevant to them.

Theresa then presents clear conflict in her email. They will be telling leaders the waiting rooms are unpleasant and patients don't want to return(!). But then, Theresa immediately follows with her BIG Idea (highlighted in bold and yellow to really call it out visually) to address the conflict: *To help reverse the downward trend, we need some "Quick Wins" that our team can implement immediately.*

This statement includes both a BENEFIT *(reverse the downward trend)* and a WHAT *(some quick wins)*. The BIG Idea that appears in the body of the email reinforces the BIG Idea that appears in the subject line. There is no ambiguity what the email is about.

Theresa is then ready to roll out her resolution, which includes the detailed action—the HOW—of the story. Her resolution is in bullet points to help her colleagues quickly scan the information and know precisely what they need to do.

And there it is, a simple email conveyed through business storytelling. Let's take a look at another example and revisit our favorite airline, Quantum, to see whether VP of People, Marco Vasquez can teach us about telling a story through email.

WHY WASTE A SENTENCE
SAYING NOTHING?

—SETH GODIN

More pilots please

When we last left Quantum Airlines in *Chapter 10: Making a Recommendation,* VP of People Marco Vasquez had laid out his recommendations to senior leadership to combat the global pilot shortage. Things must have gone well for him *(well done, Marco!)* and now, one week later, the big bosses want to know what his talent acquisition plan is going to cost. This email is a request to various members of his senior leadership team for their help in putting together an actual budget to implement these recommendations. He must submit these numbers to finance within the week. Marco needs to get his colleagues' attention quickly, and have them review all the feedback from the meeting, so that he can put together the financials.

An email that drops in from nowhere

Like many of us, Marco believed that the best way to get his email read and responded to quickly was by keeping it incredibly short. But unfortunately, his sparse language came at the expense of context, meaning, and directive. In other words, it completely skipped the storytelling. Let's take a look at what went wrong.

First and foremost, the subject line is passive: *For Budgetary Planning.* This is very generic. What budget? Plan for who? Again, the subject line is your first point of entry into your receiver's sphere of attention. *It really counts.* This is the place to introduce your BIG Idea—the WHAT that this piece of communication must express. This is the point where many readers—skimmers—might move on to something that *seems* more critical.

Next, the first line of the email fails to bring in any context to the message. It has no WHY. When Marco says: *we need a high-level budgetary plan,* he does not make it specifically clear what he means.

BEFORE STORY *What's not working?*

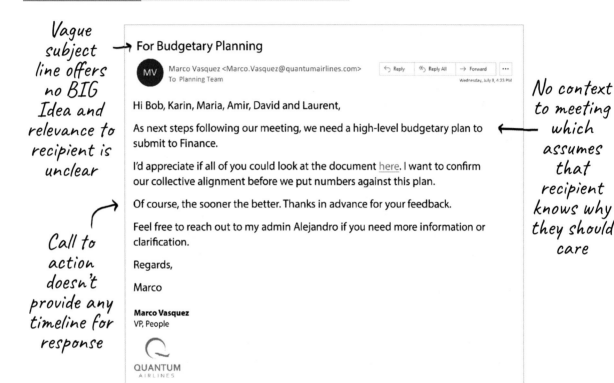

Vague subject line offers no BIG Idea and relevance to recipient is unclear

No context to meeting which assumes that recipient knows why they should care

Call to action doesn't provide any timeline for response

✗ **No BIG Idea** ✗ **No context provided** ✗ **No timeline for response**

Establishing the WHY brings everyone to the table. Without this opener, recipients (surely absorbed in something completely different as they read these words) might not remember much about the meeting they attended last week. They may scan the email and immediately be confused by who "we" is. With no background information about the meeting setting and context, they will likely set it aside and your request will rapidly get pushed down under a gazillion other requests.

Marco also missed the opportunity to remind his colleagues what prompted the recommendations—what's at stake. He's seeking to intervene with a serious problem, the pilot shortage, that will threaten the growth and future of this airline. Nowhere in this email does Marco recapture the urgency of this matter, and therefore doesn't remind them WHY they should care. Without this conflict, there is seemingly no rush on the request. And businesspeople, especially executives, constantly rank their email requests by degree of urgency.

And finally, the resolution is not clear. He asks for their "collective alignment" but that is a murky ask. His timeline of "the sooner the better" is also a recipe for disaster. You can be sure, with no clear context, specific ask, or deadline, Marco is going to find himself chasing down those replies as the week moves on. *Ugh, Marco.*

An email that grabs attention and spurs action

Now take a look at a version of this email that captures attention and will get people to respond. What do you notice first? Marco's BIG Idea pops right out in the subject line, immediately expressing what he needs his colleagues to know and do. Receivers see this right away and know WHAT this communication is about. Marco needs the team's help to build a budget by Wednesday. It grabs the reader because it clearly involves *them* and asks then to do something directly.

Click. The receiver opens the email, and *boom,* the context hits them in the first short paragraph: *Thank you for attending last week's Planning for Growth presentation where we shared HR's talent acquisition vision for the next decade. Your comments during the meeting were invaluable for further refinement and reflected in the revised version uploaded here [link to important meeting notes]. As you know, our next step is to develop a high-level budgetary recommendation for Finance's review and approval.*

AFTER STORY *What's working?*

BIG Idea
in the
subject line
specifically
calls out
what
recipients
need to know
and do

Your alignment please by Wednesday EOD to move to Budgetary Planning

} *BIG Idea*

MV Marco Vasquez <Marco.Vasquez@quantumairlines.com>   ↩ Reply   ↩ Reply All   → Forward   ···
To Planning Team   Wednesday, July 8, 4:23 PM

Hi Bob, Karin, Maria, Amir, David and Laurent,

Thank you for attending last week's *Planning for Growth* presentation where we shared HR's talent acquisition vision for the next decade. Your comments during the meeting were invaluable for further refinement and are reflected in the revised version (see below). As you know, our next step is to develop a high-level budgetary recommendation for Finance's review and approval.

} *Setting & Characters*

While the airline industry faces challenges in recovering from the recent economic downturn, Quantum, along with our competitors, will still need to compete for our fair share of pilots in the midst of continuing global shortage. Our current hiring pace won't enable us to meet growing customer demand.

} *Conflict*

BIG Idea is
repeated and
reinforced
after context
is established

To ensure we are well-positioned to double our recruiting efforts in the next decade, we need your alignment to quickly turn our recommendation into a financial investment plan.

} *BIG Idea*

Action please: Review and sign-off on this updated version by EOD on Wednesday. Please made sure:

} *Resolution*

Resolution
expressed
in bulleted
actions offers
direction to
help solve the
conflict

- All key changes we discussed have been accurately reflected
- Share any revisions/changes with the group
- Hit "Reply All" to confirm your alignment moving forward

Thanks in advance for your timely feedback! Looking forward to moving ahead to make this plan a reality.

Regards,

Marco Vasquez
VP, People

Q
QUANTUM
AIRLINES

✓ **BIG Idea in subject line**   ✓ **Begins with context**   ✓ **Resolution follows conflict**

So they attended a meeting last week *(Oh yeah, that meeting...)* where a series of recommendations were made to Quantum's senior leadership team. Now, the finance department wants to know what it's all going to cost. This lays out both setting (last week's meeting) and all the characters (the finance team, the leadership team, and of course, Marco!). With this background information established, nobody will be left wondering why they are receiving this email.

Now, just in case the reader's head is somewhere else (likely), Marco reminds them of the conflict: Quantum *must* grab their share of pilots during a global pilot shortage in order to grow. In the next line, he escalates the conflict by pointing out that their current hiring pace is just not cutting it.

Then, to address the conflict, Marco repeats the BIG Idea: to step up our recruiting in the future, we need to put some numbers to these recommendations. It includes a WHAT + a BENEFIT. Specifically he states: *To ensure we are well-positioned to double our recruiting efforts in the next decade, we need your alignment to quickly turn our recommendation into a financial investment plan.*

Let's examine this WHAT + BENEFIT statement more closely. "Ensure we are well-positioned to double our recruiting efforts" is the BENEFIT and "need your alignment..." is the WHAT. Notice how the BIG Idea in the body of the email *reinforces* the BIG Idea that appears in the subject line. This subtle repeat cements this message. Marco goes even one step further to elevate his BIG Idea by highlighting it in bold and yellow. *Powerful.*

From the BIG Idea, the email moves into the details of the resolution. Again, this is the specific action the sender is looking for from the receiver. Note how Marco uses bullet points to clearly list out what he needs. And he also injects more force into his HOW by heading his bullets with the bold words "action needed." This makes things absolutely clear that this is not some "FYI" email. This is a real plan moving forward that requires their participation.

Plow through the email blizzard

Everywhere, all the time, emails are piling into people's inboxes. Many of them never get answered. This can be demoralizing for senders and leave them baffled about what went wrong. The truth is, no one teaches us how to send a good email even though it is one of the most common things we do. It usually takes years of experience to get them right. So let's shave off some of those years by reshaping your message into the framework of a story and bringing in your WHY, WHAT, and HOW. Through this lens you will have a much better chance of pushing your message ahead of the daily email blizzard and get your ideas the attention—and response—they deserve.

CHAPTER 13

Creating a One-Pager

IMAGINE YOU SCORED A LUNCH WITH A VIP
who's willing to hear you out on a big proposal. You're not showing up
with slides and a projector, but you do want to leave her with something
to remember your ideas and influence her decision. This is where the
understated, useful one-pager comes into play. You will dine. You will
pitch. And then, you will leave behind a sheet with your key messages
and select data and facts to support it. One-pagers don't have to be
paper, they can easily be emailed or posted online as well. However
they're delivered, they should offer easy access to relevant information
with just a quick scan—a perfect follow-up to any high-stakes meeting.

THE KEY TO ONE-PAGERS IS QUICK, EASY ACCESS TO YOUR MOST RELEVANT INFORMATION.

Unfortunately, many people use one-pagers as an information dump.
They might attempt to jam the page with as many bullets as possible
in the smallest font. (Yes, technically, it's still just one page!) Others
might believe that just a few brief summary lines are best. They are
both wrong. So what's the answer? You guessed it—one-pagers are a
haven for great *storytelling*.

But how much information should you include? It's simple. When you isolate a BIG Idea—with facts and data that directly support it—and use a storytelling framework from top to bottom, the *right* amount of information will land on your page. Let's take a look at our two (by now) familiar companies, Harmony Health and Quantum Airlines, and see how well they convey their message in two versions of a one-pager.

CASE STUDY

Urgent points only for this urgent care

As you might recall, Harmony Health is in a highly competitive market for urgent care clinics. But they have a problem with patient satisfaction due to sub-par waiting rooms. There is a plan afloat to directly address the waiting room issues and improve patient satisfaction in order to ready the company to expand its network of clinics. Theresa Nielsen, Customer Experience Strategy Director, has met with the leadership team to make her recommendation (see *Chapter 10: Making a Recommendation)* and now, to further help them decide on the validity of her recommendations, she is leaving a one-pager behind (and sending it via email) as a summary of the story she presented. Let's see how she did.

BEFORE STORY *What's not working?*

HarmonyHealth
Compassionate care for all

Patient Urgent Care Plan

- We need to make improvements both in the short term (via "quick wins") and long term to establish a five star experience
- Technology needs to play a key role to help us imagine a best-in-class experience driven by innovation
- We need to involve the community by building relationships to improve access
- Online ratings for Harmony UC are low relative to our competition
- Reviews are negative with many reviewers mentioning our "dirty," "cluttered" and "messy" waiting rooms as key factor in why they don't return
- Observational field research (i.e., visits to our facilities) confirm these comments

Number of Urgent Care Centers and Industry Revenue

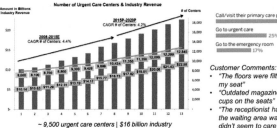

~ 9,500 urgent care centers | $16 billion industry

Call/visit their primary care provider 45%
Go to urgent care 25%
Go to the emergency room 17%

Customer Comments:
- *"The floors were filthy, gum stuck to my seat"*
- *"Outdated magazines and dirty paper cups on the seats"*
- *"The receptionist had to notice that the waiting area was a mess, but didn't seem to care"*

Solution

Solution 1: Immediate correction
- Cluster chairs to create small seating groups
- New hand sanitizer/mask dispenser and signage stations
- Replace current trash bins with hands-free automatic
- Updated purified water dispenser
- Increase waiting area cleaning cycle to twice an hour

Solution 2: Tech Solutions
- New appointment and registration app
- Optional self-serve check-in kiosks
- On-demand concierge to answer questions
- High-speed Wi-Fi and power charge stations
- For our larger centers: private workstations and dedicated quiet areas
- Test App-enabled pagers in 10 key markets

Solution 3: Community
- Partner with pharmacy for on-site prescription delivery
- Community training (CPR, home safety, hygiene, etc.)
- QR-coded digital educational materials to help inform patients on common health concerns
- Refresh video content for common medical needs/searches
- Telemedicine and virtual urgent care services

Confusing headline— this is about clinics not patients' health (plus no BIG Idea)

Data is confusing and doesn't clearly connect to anything

Resolution comes too early, before any context is set

Conflict is buried

✗ **Vague headings** ✗ **Dense data feels random** ✗ **Conflict buried deep**

Ideas are left on the table

And... we see immediate problems. Like the problem emails from *Chapter 12: Crafting an Email,* the first line—which should broadcast the BIG Idea—is missing. Instead, Theresa has headed up her one-pager with *Patient Urgent Care Plan,* a title which sounds like it's referring more to the health of patients than the clinics! Another huge problem throughout this sheet is lack of headlines. There is no logical flow of ideas from the bullets in the first third, to the data in the second third, to the solution boxes in the final third. As the eye scans from top to bottom, headlines don't help connect one idea to another, resulting in a disjointed message. Let's take a closer look at each section.

The top third of the one-pager is a hail of bullets. Immediately, the first few bullets fire off the resolution. No conflict—or any other context for that matter—greets the reader, they just go... *Boom! Here are some improvements!* The bulleted list does eventually get to some setting, characters, and conflict later down, but these background facts would have made much more sense *before* the resolution was stated.

In the second third of the one-pager, broader market data is dumped onto the page. The charts offer no obvious information about how they support a BIG Idea (which by the way, has yet to be introduced).

The data in the second third of the one-pager is unclear. In addition to lack of headlines, it's also difficult to pick up any meaningful insights from the charts. The vague title *Number of Urgent Care Centers and Industry Revenue* tells us nothing. Remember, the goal of a one-pager is to educate the viewer in one glance—these charts do the opposite. They *appear* to be establishing setting and characters to show the broader market, but they are too confusing to be much help. The second section does reveal the data about negative patient reviews—a key part of the conflict—but this information is *begging* for a headline to alert the viewer of its tremendous significance.

In the final third, the three solution boxes are clearly part of the resolution, but the section is so jammed with bullets, it's difficult to read. Eyes are surely glazing over.

Everything about this one-pager, from the "information-dump" layout to the lack of flow between each section, makes it more difficult to grasp Theresa's ideas than less. (And this defeats the whole purpose of a one-pager.) Without a doubt, this document can be improved with a story framework that will guide readers through a logical flow of ideas and help them quickly understand what they need to know and do. Time for a makeover.

A page that educates quickly

Well hello, BIG Idea! *This* is what we're talking about. Notice how the BIG Idea anchors this one-pager and blazes the key message right from the first place that the eye settles: *Patient care starts with facility care: To deliver exceptional experience we need to create an inviting space.*

Unlike the previous version, it is now clear that this one-pager is not about the state of Harmony's patients' health but about the state of Harmony's facilities. Very different! This BIG Idea includes a WHAT and a BENEFIT that immediately tells the reader what she needs to know.

The next section launches into setting and characters which provide context about the overall care preferences of patients in the market. Bottom line, it shows that the market offers them plenty of choices. This carefully selected data tees up the conflict that is about to come.

The next section, using a clear, *active* headline, explicitly spells out the conflict. Adjacent data escalates the conflict by showing the negative

AFTER STORY *What's working?*

Big Idea is a headline blazing from the top of the page →

Select data shows setting and characters →

Hint of conflict tees up the section below

Resolution comes last and put into clear, visual "buckets" →

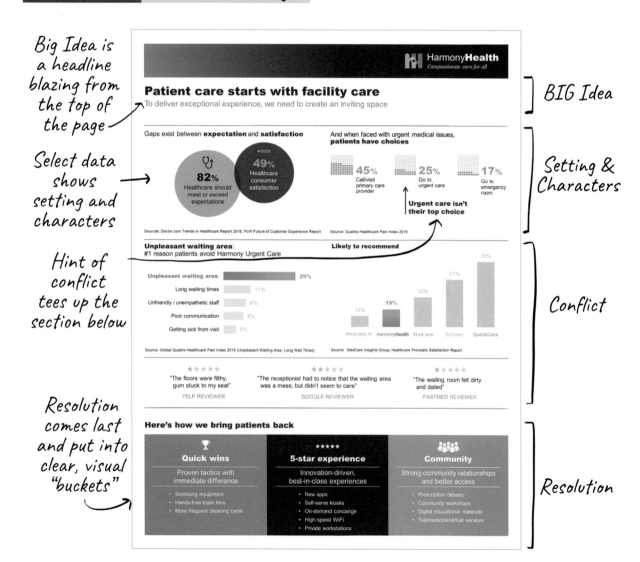

HarmonyHealth
Compassionate care for all

Patient care starts with facility care
To deliver exceptional experience, we need to create an inviting space

Gaps exist between **expectation** and **satisfaction**

82% Healthcare should meet or exceed expectations

49% Healthcare consumer satisfaction

And when faced with urgent medical issues, **patients have choices**

45% Call/visit primary care provider

25% Go to urgent care

17% Go to emergency room

Urgent care isn't their top choice

Sources: Doctor.com Trends in Healthcare Report 2018; PcW Future of Customer Experience Report

Source: Qualtrix Healthcare Pain Index 2019

Unpleasant waiting area:
#1 reason patients avoid Harmony Urgent Care

Unpleasant waiting area	29%
Long waiting times	11%
Unfriendly / unempathetic staff	9%
Poor communication	8%
Getting sick from visit	5%

Likely to recommend

SPEED HEALTH 12% | HarmonyHealth 19% | WeCare 32% | DrZoom 51% | QuickCare 70%

Source: Global Qualtrix Healthcare Pain Index 2019 (Unpleasant Waiting Area, Long Wait Times)

Source: MedCare Insights Group, Healthcare Providers Satisfaction Report

★☆☆☆☆ "The floors were filthy, gum stuck to my seat" YELP REVIEWER

★★☆☆☆ "The receptionist had to notice that the waiting area was a mess, but didn't seem to care" GOOGLE REVIEWER

★☆☆☆☆ "The waiting room felt dirty and dated" FASTMED REVIEWER

Here's how we bring patients back

🏆 **Quick wins**	★★★★★ **5-star experience**	👥 **Community**
Proven tactics with immediate difference	Innovation-driven, best-in-class experiences	Strong community relationships and better access
• Sanitizing equipment • Hands-free trash bins • More frequent cleaning cycle	• New apps • Self-serve kiosks • On-demand concierge • High-speed WiFi • Private workstations	• Prescription delivery • Community workshops • Digital educational materials • Telemedicine/virtual services

BIG Idea

Setting & Characters

Conflict

Resolution

✓ **BIG Idea is prominent at top** ✓ **Context and conflict come next** ✓ **Resolution is easy to scan**

opinion that current patients have about Harmony's clinics. They don't like the waiting rooms, and judging by Harmony's measly market share, *this matters.* The problem is now leaping off the page.

And then in the final section, the one-pager launches into the resolution: *Here's how we are going to bring patients back.*

Each resolution is clear and maps directly back to the conflict that was previously established. The impact of all of this is further increased by simple design tricks of color, "bucketized" information, and a very controlled volume of text. (Yes, there are bullets... but only a few.) Finally, since it is unnecessary to repeat the BIG Idea after the conflict is stated in a one-pager, this message is reinforced in the headline of the resolution: *Patient care starts with facility care.*

And that is a story told in one page. Let's take a look at another example.

WRITING IS 1% INSPIRATION

AND 99% ELIMINATION

—LOUISE BROOKS

CASE STUDY

A story lost in flight

Hello again, Quantum Airlines (from *Chapter 10: Making a Recommendation)* and our busy VP of People Marco Vasquez. Here is the one-pager that Marco left behind after his big presentation to his leadership team. Remember, he just offered recommendations on how Quantum should address the global pilot shortage that will hamper the company's growth. He wants to leave his key points with the team to help them decide on his recommendations. Let's see how he did with his first one-pager attempt.

Marco has some serious problems.

Let's take his vague headline: *Future Growth Planning* (or should we say heading, because a headline implies actual news). Just... no. This boring heading incites no curiosity about the rest of this page, nor would it trigger much memory about his recommendations or why he was making them. To attract attention and trigger recall, this top-of-the-page real estate should *broadcast* his BIG Idea. Moving on.

The first section of his one-pager is (you guessed it) all resolution. He immediately jumps in with his densely worded recruitment plan. This is problematic because the one-pager should be providing a quick refresher on the whole presentation. If someone on the leadership teams scans this sheet a few days later, his resolution will not be meaningful. They need context through setting, characters, and conflict in order to fully remember why his resolutions are valuable.

The second section throws in some data. It *could* have been useful as context (particularly if it came before the resolution) except that there is no connection forged between the data and the preceding section

BEFORE STORY *What's not working?*

Vague heading doesn't capture BIG Idea

Story begins with resolution before setting and characters have been introduced— why should anyone care?

Setting and characters come after resolution (which is too late) and data doesn't make sense

Future Growth Planning

Our Recruitment Plan

Candidate Outreach Efforts
- Develop mentorship program to ensure that newly hired pilots are ready to work and fly with Quantum
- Implement new screening and selection process which we will develop in the next 6-12 months
- Groom future potential captains through training and mentorship
- Launch new training that is adaptive, data-driven and customized
- Implement new competency gap and pilot performance assessment

Targeting Female Pilots
- Today, women account for approximately 5.4% of airline commercial pilots globally
- Increase the number of female pilots we to attract future candidates hire
- Create more female-friendly schedule, culture and working policies
- Develop outreach and flight training sponsorship program
- Role model and engage girls through STEM program early

Attracting Future Candidates
- Partner with CAE, major aviation colleges and universities to develop flight academy program and curricula
- Subsidize or sponsor recruits who are high-potential
- Partner with banks to provide financing options and low-interest aviation student loans
- Implement new compensation and signing bonus model as further incentive
- Launch pre-hire onboarding program so they get up-to-speed quickly

Number of New Pilots Needed in Next Decade

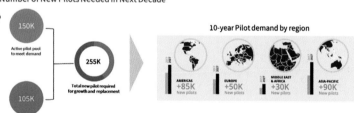

Rationale for Our Plan

GROWTH
- Passenger numbers are forecast to double from 2010 to 2030; i.e., 3.5% CAGR
- In 2000, the average citizen flew just once every 43 months. In 2017, the figure was once every 22 months
- Growth will come from Asia

PILOT COMPOSITION
- 50% of pilots flying by 2027 have not yet started to train
- In the U.S., women account for 12% of pilot students, showing a strong upward trend
- From 2003 to 2016, 35% fewer students completed academic programs for airline/commercial/professional pilot and flight crew
- To complete a commercial aviation program and flight hours to qualify costs $125K on average

✗ **No BIG Idea** ✗ **Story begins with resolution** ✗ **Context comes too late**

or the story at large. It feels random. The reader may wonder why it is included and how the number of pilots the world needs in the next decade (by region as well!) relates to Quantum. Would a smart leader figure out this connection? Sure. But if Marco wants this one-pager to be an easy refresher following his big meeting from a few days ago, the connection should be made obvious—no extra work for the reader. Oh boy, the value of this one-pager is diving fast.

The final section, which attempts to offer rationale for his recommendations, comes in at totally the wrong place. This section should have been introduced first because it establishes setting and characters that build the crucial WHY of the story. These bullets, with all kinds of supportive facts and figures, come too late in the story to offer meaning. The reader will be forced to scan upwards again (at the conflict and resolution) to make sense of anything.

Let's see if Marco can take another shot at his one-pager so that the team can scan it quickly, top to bottom, and instantly understand the logical flow of his story.

One page. One scannable story.

Hallelujah! Right off the bat, Marco's BIG Idea blazes from the top headline. Since this is where eyes go first, the WHAT of this story is clear right from the beginning: *Robust pilot strategy ensures we're not left at the gate. We need to secure our share of pilots to secure our future.*

It specifically says that his story is about hiring pilots (not future growth strategy).

From there, Marco puts his story signposts in the right order. First, he brings out setting and characters to provide context, which he then backs up with relevant, supportive data. Passengers (characters) will

AFTER STORY *What's working?*

Powerful headline spells out the story's BIG Idea

BIG Idea [

Setting and characters set the stage and build to the conflict

Active headlines advance the story forward

Resolution is easy to scan and comes last

Setting & Characters

Conflict

Resolution

✓ **BIG Idea at top** ✓ **Active headlines throughout** ✓ **Easy-to-scan resolution**

double by 2040, led by Asia (setting) with India (setting) showing the biggest increase of all.

In the second section, he brings in the pilot shortage (conflict) that threatens all airlines. Again, he chooses very select data to support this conflict. As the eye moves from left to right, he escalates the conflict with another chart of pilot needs for the entire industry. He powerfully captions the data by stating Quantum's conflict in terms of what they must do to keep up with growth: *This doubles our past recruiting efforts.*

In the final section he offers three resolutions. This time, they arrive at the *right* time. The reader has felt the pilot shortage concern and is ready to take his recommendations seriously. Marco does a great job of breaking each resolution down into easy-to-read buckets that draw separate focus to each one. Like the Harmony Health one-pager, this sheet uses the headline in the resolution to reinforce the BIG Idea. He's made it clear that Quantum needs new talent and he has a plan to win them. *Bravo Marco!*

IN SHORT...

When one page must say it all

Whether you are dining with a sales prospect, making recommendations to your executive team, or just want to keep your message top of mind, a simple one-pager can be exactly what you need to reinforce your ideas. It's brief, it's filled with your key messages, and it's easy to leave behind (or email). But in order to make sure it remains valuable to the reader, it must be scannable and easy to digest. Mold your ideas to a story framework and—like any recommendation, update, or email—this will give decision-makers the easiest access to them... in just one page. Magic.

RECAP

Everyday Storytelling

RECOMMENDATIONS, UPDATES, AND EMAILS

Business storytelling is most useful when it transforms and strengthens our common, everyday communications.

1

Making recommendations

All recommendations must start with context (your WHY), built with a setting, character, and conflict. *This* is why decision-makers will care about your recommendation/resolution (or your HOW). Just before you dive into those recommendations, drop in your critical BIG Idea to cement the WHAT of your story.

2

Providing updates

Updates are an opportunity to show your command of a project, coming either with or without conflict. With conflict, use your baseline story structure (WHY, WHAT, HOW) to reveal and resolve the issue. No conflict? Then you'll only need to introduce a few story elements (setting, characters, and a BIG Idea).

3

Crafting email

Every email is an opportunity to tell a story. Keep it lean but inject meaning with a baseline story structure—your BIG Idea is the subject line. Always start with context (setting, characters, conflict) and end with a resolution. Be clear about the recipient's role and action required for faster response.

4

Building one-pagers

One-pagers leave decision-makers with your key points following a high-stakes meeting. Never jam them with too much information or data. Clean sections should include your BIG Idea (starting at the top), followed by the four story signposts, all anchored by active headlines that flow from one to another.

PART 5

But wait!

How Do I Flex My Story?

CHAPTER 14

Audience Is Everything: A Manifesto

JUST KIDDING, this is *not* a manifesto. But, gather around, and let's have a frank talk about the people you interact with every day. Let's talk about your boss, your staff, your customer, your investor, your partners, you know... the people who might be on the receiving end of your ideas. For all of their sake, hear these words:

The best storytellers step outside of their world and *walk in their audience's shoes.*

When you approach your story—or any presentation of ideas—think about who your audience is and what is their mindset. Ask these three questions: *What's happening in their world? Who or what matters to them? What challenge(s) are they facing?*

Because no matter what *you* believe is a fantastic story, your audience will more likely be riveted by the story if *it's about them.* And given that you are hoping to move, change, or inspire *them,* theirs is the opinion that matters. You must give them what they need.

It's not about you. It's always about your audience.

THE BEST STORYTELLERS STEP
OUTSIDE OF THEIR WORLD AND
WALK IN THEIR AUDIENCE'S SHOES

Now, none of this focus-on-your-audience advice should be too surprising. After all, we spend most of our time at work trying to convince audiences (especially decision-makers) to *do* things—to get them to say "yes."

But late at night in a hotel room, while we're frantically trying to cobble together slides for an 8 a.m. presentation, we can easily lose sight of our audience. And this is when we end up with that incoherent hodgepodge of slides we call the *Frankendeck.*

So, how do you avoid building a *Frankendeck?* Have a well-established process—baked right into the development of your story—that will ensure you have done adequate due diligence on your audience's needs.

Your audience's perspective is shaped by their role

People who serve in different roles and at different levels have strikingly varied perspectives. And it is well worth your time to understand these different perspectives because it affects how they will react to and interact with your story (which could very well impact the messages you choose to emphasize).

Are you facing executives and key stakeholders? Mid-level managers? Individual contributors? Each has a totally different set of needs and priorities.

Executives are there to approve

Time-crunched executives and key stakeholders spend most of their day approving things. And with their big-picture mindset, they're obsessed with weighing benefits vs. risks, longer-term strategic impact, and of course, required investment.

Managers can help influence

Mid-level managers might not be red or green-lighting decisions all day long but they are in a position of influence. If they like your ideas, there's a good chance they'll spread them. They're also focused on how your ideas will affect day-to-day strategy and how success will be measured.

Individual contributors make it happen

Those who are on the ground executing your ideas care about what's in it for them. Individual contributors are interested in how your recommendation will impact their day-to-day operations.

THE MORE YOUR STORY ADDRESSES YOUR AUDIENCE'S UNIQUE PERSPECTIVE, THE MORE RELEVANT IT WILL FEEL TO THEM.

Digging for dirt on your audience

So how do you really learn about your audience's perspective? You need to put your *Sherlock* cap on. Let's go back and revisit the three questions we introduced at the beginning of this chapter:

✓ *What's happening in your audience's world?*

✓ *Who or what do they care about?*

✓ *What challenges are they currently facing?*

Answers to these questions will lead you to your story's WHY. Let's take a look at how each question relates to the first three signposts.

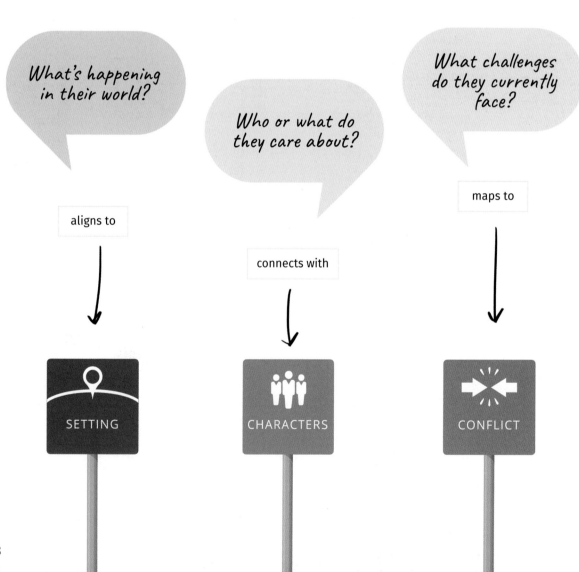

AUDIENCES VARY
TREMENDOUSLY

ONE SIZE DOES NOT FIT ALL

So, how do I adapt my story for different audiences?

Knowing that every audience has different needs, it's up to you to figure out *who* you are talking to and adapt your story to address their needs. This means you may need to move around, expand, or contract elements of your story to suit your audience. In short, you'll need to flex your story.

To see how simple it is to flex your story, let's revisit the baseline story structure

Remember, all great stories have a WHY, a WHAT, and a HOW. The WHY is established alongside your first three signposts: setting, characters, and conflict (in any order you choose). This is where you are laying out the *context* of your story and giving your audience a reason to care. The WHAT is your BIG Idea—your most crucial point or key "take-home"—and the one thing your audience *must* remember from your story. The HOW is your resolution: your recommendation, solution overview, proposal, etc.

A LOOK AHEAD

To get an idea of how you can flex your story to suit different audiences, let's stop... and teleport ourselves straight to the office. In the next chapter, we'll look at some oh-so-familiar meeting scenarios that we've all faced at one point or another.

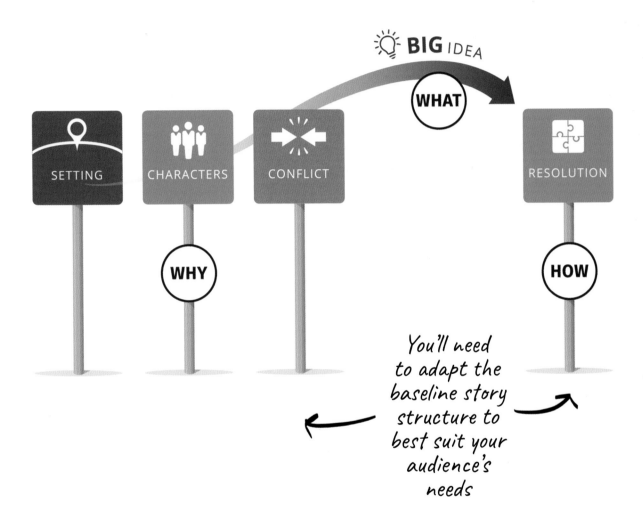

You'll need to adapt the baseline story structure to best suit your audience's needs

CHAPTER 15

You've Got Five Minutes with an Executive... Go!

IMAGINE YOUR TEAM has spent weeks preparing to deliver a huge proposal. You've spent countless hours researching the executive team you're about to face. Everyone is already on edge, hoping to nail the tightly scripted, 30-minute presentation. If you land this deal, you're all looking *real good.*

Except, the team of senior executives you are about to wow... is running late.

You now have five minutes.

So, what do you do? How do you cram 30 minutes of awesomeness into five minutes?

This is a common scenario we should be prepared for, always. After all, we know executives are often short on time, short on attention, and sometimes even short-tempered! You should always be prepared for the unexpected.

Let's take a look at how to adapt your baseline story structure so that you can instantly respond to the dreadful vanishing time scenario.

Introducing the pivot strategy

What's the latest business dance craze? It's called **the pivot**™. When you address executives—or any key stakeholder—you need to be flexible to pivot to their needs. Using the core story structure as your foundation, begin with your BIG Idea (remember, it's the WHAT of your story) and pay attention to the feedback you are receiving from your audience. If you receive a request for *more* context, back up and offer the setting, character, and conflict of your story (the WHY). This can be done verbally or visually. It will be a *very* brief background explanation.

But, if your executive or key stakeholder is impatient to push onto the resolution (meaning, if they accept your BIG Idea without requesting more context) you can move ahead to your HOW—the resolution. Remember, your resolution is where you hit them with your concrete plan and have details ready upon request.

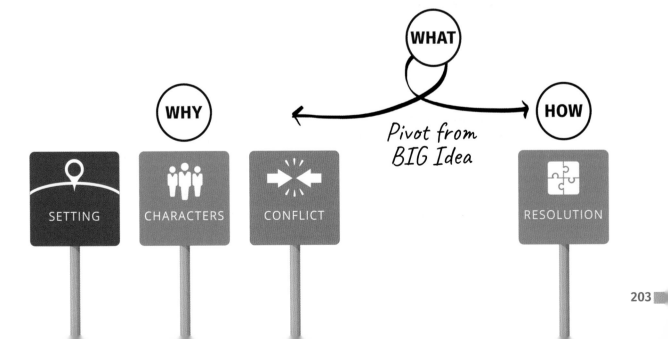

The pivot isn't hard, but you must know your story well and be flexible

It goes without saying, to do the pivot right, you have to know your story backwards and forwards. One of the most important skills you can learn is flexibility. Yes, you've prepared a well-ordered, well-constructed story, but you must also be prepared to get thrown off course.

YOU MUST ALWAYS BE READY TO TELL YOUR STORY OUT OF SEQUENCE OR NONLINEARLY.

Depending on the needs of your audience, you'll have to zig and zag, go back and forth, drill down, or stay high level. To keep you (and your audience) oriented in your story, all you need is an anchor point—a home base, if you will—from which to pivot. That anchor point is always your BIG Idea.

Take a cue from your audience

Being ready to pivot is great, but this does not mean you should skip important elements of your story. As mentioned earlier, establishing your setting, characters, and conflict is how you hook your audience. It's how you get them to care. Even if you have just minutes to present, you should, at a bare minimum, take 30–60 seconds to verbally establish some context—the WHY of your story. If, however, you are facing people who are already very familiar with the context of your story, you need to hit your BIG Idea and then, quickly, move to your resolution.

Flex your story intact... don't shred it

Let's take a look at how the pivot strategy affects your slide deck (if you're telling your story visually in a presentation). The good news is that your original, linear story remains intact. There is no need to delete or move any slides around. The trick is to simply hide the slides that you want to skip so that you can spotlight exactly what your audience is interested in. But again, in the case of the five-minute rush story, you'll begin with your BIG Idea slide.

Hidden slides, hyperlinks, and landing pages, oh my!

Nimble storytellers require a few simple skills and tools. To properly pivot in your story, you need to know how to hide slides so that *you* can see them, but your audience can't. Therefore, during your meeting, you can jump around in your deck without having to fumble through unnecessary visuals.

BEHIND THE SCENES, HIDDEN SLIDES ALLOW YOU TO CONTROL WHAT YOUR AUDIENCE SEES.

If you suddenly need to jump to the end, you don't need to click through every slide in your linear story to get there. This is best pulled off with a landing page that includes hyperlinks to other parts of the presentation—kind of like a homepage.

CASE STUDY

The pivot strategy in action

Let's examine the pivot strategy in the context of our insurance story (that we introduced in earlier chapters) to show how it works at the slide level. As you might recall, this story involves reaching new insurance shoppers. If you had to present this story in a time crunch, you might not have time to show your WHY slides. Instead, you will first lay down your BIG Idea: "To reach tomorrow's insurance shoppers, we need to build relevance during their buying journey." From there, you would *pause* and ask for feedback from your audience.

You'll want to ask: *"Would you like to know why we need to build relevance with younger generations of insurance shoppers? Or, would you like to know how we're going to build relevance?"*

You're probing to find out if they want more background (WHY) or just want to jump ahead to the execution (HOW). When you receive their response, you will pivot to their needs immediately.

ALWAYS MOVE ACCORDING TO YOUR AUDIENCE'S RESPONSE.

**Create a dialogue with your audience and
give them control over the flow of information**

Do they need more detail about today's insurance market?

Do they want data about how people are currently purchasing insurance?

Do they want to know why our old marketing methods aren't working anymore?

Do they want to skip ahead to the solution and see how to reach new insurance buyers?

Show your setting slide

Hello, characters!

Jump to conflict

Skip right to your resolution

SETTING

CHARACTERS

CONFLICT

RESOLUTION

Structurally, the story remains intact, in a linear order. Why? So that you don't have to create multiple versions of the same story *(hello, time saver!)* The difference now is that everything is hidden, except your BIG Idea slide, where you begin. Nothing else appears until you click on a hyperlink to drill deeper. In other words, you are set up to go in any direction from your "home base" (your BIG Idea).

Asking your audience where they want to go is a smart strategy. You are putting your audience in the driver's seat! Audiences love this—especially executives.

Pivot from BIG Idea based on audience's feedback

Giving up control... to get control

The pivot strategy might seem complicated to some, but actually, it puts you in control of your story. Anything that can turn meetings and conversations into two-way dialogues—rather than monologues—shows off your mastery of the material and your executive presence.

WHEN YOU'RE ABLE TO ADJUST AND HELP EXECUTIVES MAKE QUICK DECISIONS, IT MAKES *YOU* APPEAR MORE CREDIBLE.

Your value will soar in the eyes of your boss, your customer, your team, or whomever you face when you prove that you understand their world. Pivoting is a winning strategy because it prevents you from getting flustered when unexpected things happen like your time getting cut short or someone in your audience going off on a tangent (sound familiar?). In fact, at the multinational and Fortune 500 companies we train, we've seen even the most introverted and nervous presenters increase their confidence and truly "own the room" with the pivot strategy.

CHAPTER 16

Your Audience Is Diverse...

How can you please everyone?

WHAT IF YOUR AUDIENCE IS MIXED, comprised of people serving different functions, with competing interests, and varying levels of knowledge? You can't possibly address *everyone's* needs with the same story, right?

Actually, you can.

This is a very common scenario. And similar to the pivot strategy, you'll need to adjust your baseline story structure. You'll keep the key elements and structure intact but in the case of a diverse audience, your story must actually grow.

Your incredible growing story

First, you must consider all the major constituencies in your audience. If you want to address the needs of each of these interest groups, you'll need to introduce multiple characters into your story. And each character will likely face their own unique conflict. Why? Because each conflict will have particular significance to each group.

Now in some stories, you *may* be able to find one common conflict that everyone in your audience shares, but this approach is often tricky and more often, unlikely. So for the most part, with diverse audiences, be prepared to introduce multiple characters and conflicts. However, you will only ever have one, overarching BIG Idea.

ONE BIG IDEA MUST UNITE EVERYONE AND EVERYTHING IN YOUR STORY.

Let's say you're trying to push a brand-new service idea to the C-Suite at your company. Pam the CTO wants to hear pure technical specs. Robert in HR is primarily interested in how many new hires the initiative will require. Maria the CFO is laser-focused on which P&L this new service will fall under. Yes, you have one audience, but in actuality, you are facing (at least) three.

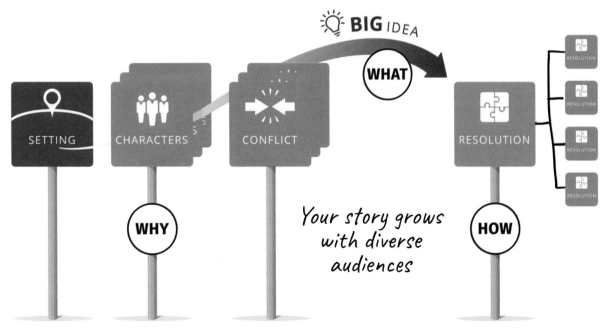

From your slightly inflated WHY (setting, characters, and conflict), you will move to the HOW (your resolution). And here, we recommend using a landing page to segment your resolution into clear paths. Each of these paths resolves each conflict you have introduced. And again, each of these conflicts maps directly to the various needs of your diverse audience.

And of course, always remain flexible and seek interaction with your audience. Never assume you must present everything in a linear fashion. This is particularly true with diverse audiences because you can be sure all those different people will be interested in different details of your story.

CASE STUDY

Selling laptops in schools

A participant in one of our corporate storytelling workshops—a sales manager for a large computer hardware company—brought in a perfect example of a challenging, diverse audience. She sells technology solutions to the education sector (think laptops, desktops, workstations, and digital devices built for learning, and tough enough to survive in the classroom). When she approaches schools, her audience is always extremely mixed. She pitches to a roomful of teachers, IT folks, and school board members, all of whom have unique needs and concerns. She can not rely on a "one-size-fits-all" story for this audience. To make her case, she has to address their *individual* needs up front.

For the story's WHY, *unnamed* characters are introduced

"For educators, we know you have limited time and resources. For IT, we know you want secure technology that's easy to implement and maintain. And for the school board, we know you face limited district funding."

Named characters work well too

Meet Joe, Alex, and Maria

Here's how the story's WHY (using named characters) came alive visually

"Joe is a third grade teacher. He wants to implement technology in his classroom but has limited time and is resource constrained. Alex runs the IT department at a middle school. He cares about secure technology that he can efficiently manage. Maria is on the school board. She too wants to see technology in the classroom, but with limited district funding, she must heavily weigh the costs and benefits. Collectively, Joe, Alex, and Maria want the same thing: Affordable, flexible and user-friendly technology in the classroom."

Setting, Characters & Conflict

From the story's WHY, we move to the WHAT (the BIG Idea)

After she unveils her characters—be they named or unnamed—along with their conflicts, she hits the audience with her BIG Idea: *Affordable, flexible, and user-friendly technology in the classroom leads to active, inspired learners.* Notice how she doesn't have three BIG Ideas. Instead, she has one BIG Idea that unites everyone in her audience. That's by design. You can only have one BIG Idea in your story, otherwise your audience won't remember the *one thing* you want them to know or do afterwards.

From the BIG Idea, the resolution is previewed

Now that the story's WHY and WHAT have been clearly established, she's ready to reveal her HOW, the resolution. To anchor her story, she uses a landing page to show the multiple facets of her resolution. It's a map of each way her solution will address the conflicts facing each constituency. The landing page allows her to easily drill into each of these separate solutions.

A landing page sparks conversation

Landing pages are a clever solution for a multi-pronged story like this one because it is easy for both the presenter and audience to see where details are available for drill-down. It shows clearly where the conversation is prepared to go.

Landing page

Drill-down slides

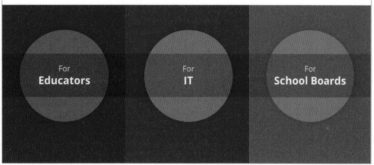

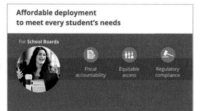

Resolution

Drill-down slides provide more detail

You can have as many or as few resolution drill-down slides as you need. In this example, there's only one slide per each solution (to convey the concept here), but in reality, you might have several "behind the curtain" slides to support your HOW.

CHAPTER 17

You're Told "Only Three to Five Slides"

THIS IS A TOUGH SITUATION that is *extremely* common. For whatever reason—company culture, policy, time constraints—you must tell your story in just a few slides.

Perhaps your boss has asked you to choose *just three slides* so that she can present a team idea to *her* boss. You have two challenges. First, you must truncate your baseline story to *get to your point quickly* and second, you must prepare your story to be easily delivered by someone else. So, what do you do? (And no, the answer isn't to decrease the font size!)

There are two good options for telling your story in only three to five slides. Option 1: you present your WHY verbally, or option 2: show your WHY visually on just one slide. If your boss is presenting the story for you, you've got to decide if you can rely on her or him to verbally establish the WHY or if she'll need the visual cue of the one slide. In other words, how much of a control freak do you need to be about your story?

Let's take a closer look at both options.

Option 1: Present your WHY verbally

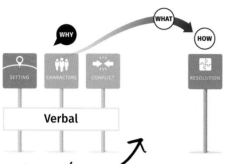

In this scenario, you establish the setting, characters, and conflict of your story verbally, then you show your WHAT (remember, this is your BIG Idea). After you've visually presented your BIG Idea, you can proceed to show your HOW (your resolution). You've only got a few slides, so be sure to keep the details to a minimum.

Option 1 works great if you (or someone you know and trust) are the storyteller

Option 1 works great if you (or someone you know and trust) are the storyteller. In other words, you have total confidence that the WHY of your story will be delivered "on message" and the way you intended. But if you've got any doubt, option 2 is a safer choice.

Option 2: Show your WHY visually

In this scenario, you will need one slide (yes, only one!) to visually show your WHY. Now, we're not going to lie... truncating all of that context onto *one slide* can be tough! You must only include *the* most relevant points. But if everything you include supports your BIG Idea, and you've left the extraneous stuff out, you should be in good shape.

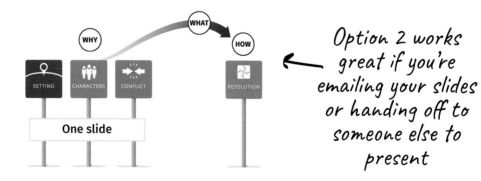

Option 2 works great if you're emailing your slides or handing off to someone else to present

In our GO Insurance story, see how the WHY is established on one slide, the WHAT is displayed on one slide, and finally, the HOW is kept to just two to three slides.

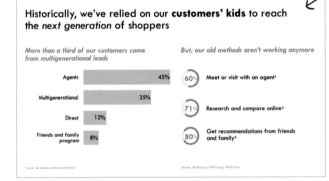

Note that the headline captures the conflict of the story

The WHY is simplified onto one slide

The WHAT is a simple statement— your BIG Idea

The HOW—your resolution—comes last

CHAPTER 18

Team Presentations: Who Does What?

DO YOU WORK ON A TEAM? We're guessing yes. Doesn't everybody at some point in their career end up working on a team? And with your colleagues, you've probably been faced with some kind of high-stakes meeting or presentation, which can turn out to be highly rewarding... *or utterly painful.*

Team collaboration is great when it draws on the varied talents of multiple people—a brain trust—who all contribute in their own way. But the drawback? Having a bunch of talented contributors all trying to tell a different story, resulting in a cobbled-together "hot mess." (For more on this scenario, review *Chapter 9: Five Well-Tested Ways to Visualize Your Story* which describes that scary, mash-up, composition known as a *Frankendeck*.)

But team storytelling doesn't have to be messy. It's very possible for even *large* teams to co-build a strong, cohesive narrative and deliver it visually, verbally, or some combination of both.

TO AVOID A RAMBLING, AUDIENCE-CONFUSING MESS, YOUR TEAM NEEDS A PLAN *AND A PROCESS* TO BUILD AND DELIVER A COMMUNAL STORY.

And part of that process is always to focus on story first, visuals second. No matter how tempting it is, never open PowerPoint (or any other visualization program) until you have your story down pat.

Let's talk first about the build.

Building together, then apart, then together

In the beginning of the build, the team must collaborate on three main things: the WHY of the story (remember, this is the setting, characters, and conflict), the WHAT (the BIG Idea), and the high-level preview of the HOW (the resolution).

Building a team story

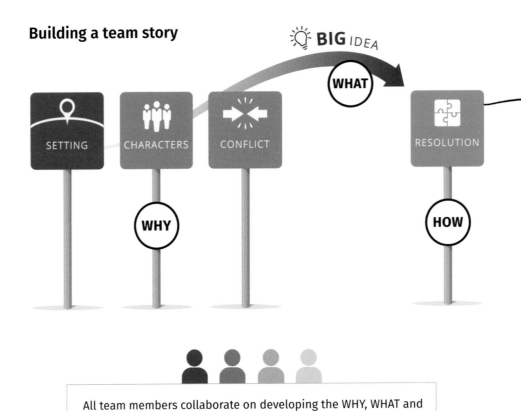

All team members collaborate on developing the WHY, WHAT and *preview* of the HOW to ensure all perspectives are included

The team must agree on these pieces because—as we constantly find in our corporate storytelling workshops—this is the most iterative part of the process. As two, three, four, or more people build a story using the framework, they riff off one another to hammer out the building blocks of the story. What is plainly obvious to see? When they all stick to a common framework, they can align quickly.

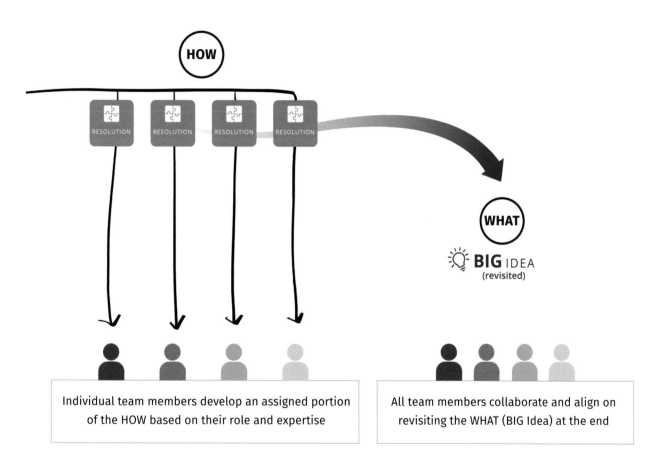

Individual team members develop an assigned portion of the HOW based on their role and expertise

All team members collaborate and align on revisiting the WHAT (BIG Idea) at the end

After carefully considering their audience, the team must decide how to establish the setting, introduce the characters, and reveal the conflict to really get them to care about their resolution. And as we discussed in *Chapter 16: Your Audience Is Diverse... How Can You Please Everyone?* this requires a serious look at the multiple perspectives your audience might have.

Once your team (enthusiastically) agrees on the WHY and the WHAT, you can move on to the preview of the HOW. This preview is where you introduce the different paths you will take to solve the conflict. Think of it like the 30,000-foot view of your resolution.

Building this preview—again, a highly iterative process—is what readies the team to branch off into separate areas to work individually.

In a business presentation, this preview can be accomplished with a landing page that visually "bucketizes" each part of the resolution (we recommend anywhere between three and five buckets).

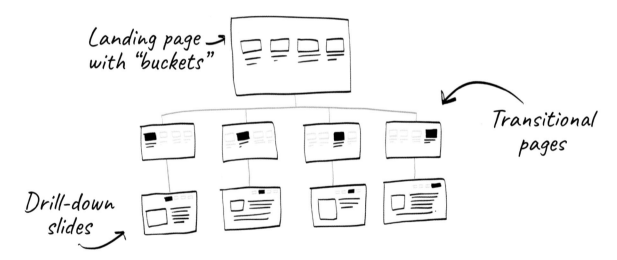

Landing page with "buckets"

Transitional pages

Drill-down slides

When the buckets for the landing page are established, the team can split them up and individually build out their portion of the story's resolution. At this point, everyone is equipped to build on their own since they all took part in creating the framework of the story. In particular, having collaborated on the conflict of the story, gives everyone a precise target to aim *their* part of the resolution. They must also be mindful of the BIG Idea, carrying it forward, right through to the end. Team members are also well-equipped to refer back to the setting and characters for context, to draw references, and of course, always connect the dots between the headlines.

A LANDING PAGE LETS EACH SPEAKER DRILL INTO THEIR CONTENT (AND HAND OFF TO THE NEXT) WITHOUT LOSING FLOW.

The through-line can easily get lost in storytelling. But for team storytelling, there is constant concern about one or more people going off on a tangent. Collaborating on each of these pieces, the WHY, the WHAT, and the preview of the HOW will ensure that everyone stays mindful of the part they are playing in the larger collaborative "dance" of the narrative.

So how do you wrap up the story build? Always together. The team must reassemble to join their pieces and make sure they all lead back to the (oft-repeated) BIG Idea. And, if you recall in *Chapter 8: A Simple Path to Building Your BIG Idea,* the BIG Idea which was established as a longer WHAT/BENEFIT statement might finish a bit snappier, more like a soundbite to end things with a flourish.

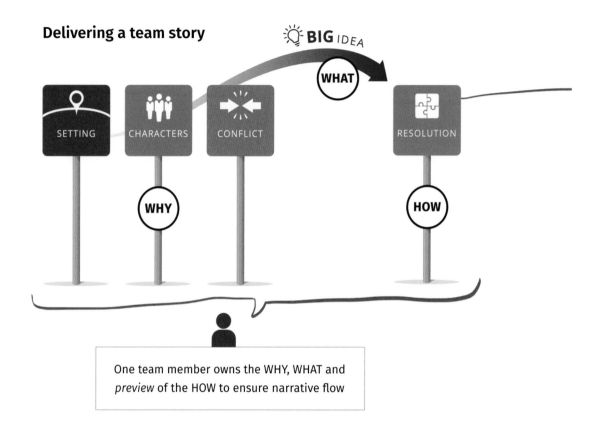

Delivering a team story

One team member owns the WHY, WHAT and *preview* of the HOW to ensure narrative flow

Now it's time to dance

We refer to delivering team stories as a "dance" because they require *choreography.*

As we mentioned, in the building phase, the team works *together* to establish the WHY and WHAT of the story. Then they can work individually on the HOW—the resolution. Finally, they come together at the end to make sure it all connects together.

The delivery of the team story is flipped. The story is introduced by a solo dancer—the host or emcee of the presentation. Their job is to

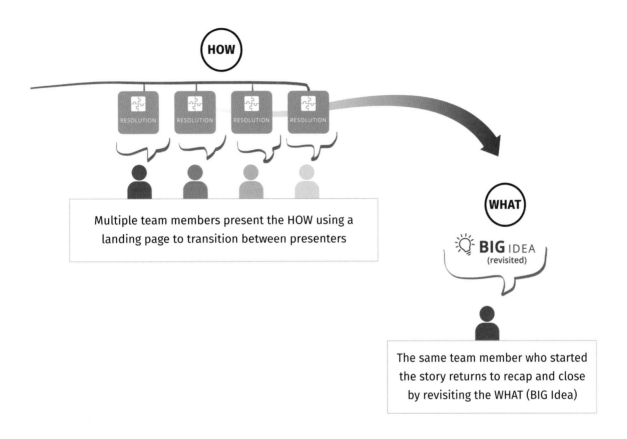

Multiple team members present the HOW using a landing page to transition between presenters

The same team member who started the story returns to recap and close by revisiting the WHAT (BIG Idea)

build up the context, introducing the WHY (setting, characters, and conflict), the WHAT (BIG Idea), and *preview* the HOW (this is where the landing page comes in handy). Then the other members of the team show up with their individual "HOWS." And finally, the solo dancer appears again, reiterating the BIG Idea and closing out the presentation. This carefully choreographed "dance" ensures all story elements flow with minimal distraction between speakers. It works beautifully for teams delivering a story in person or online, with visuals or without.

Let's see how a real team story is built and delivered.

Who does what?

01
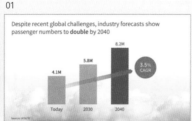

02

Setting & Characters

Marco delivers the WHY

06

07

08

Resolution

Marco previews the HOW
with a landing page

Transitional landing page is shown
to handoff between speakers

Charlie drills down into the
first resolution bucket

12

13

14

Resolution

BIG Idea

Michelle drills down into the
third resolution bucket

Review of resolution and final
handoff between speakers

Marco revisits Big Idea

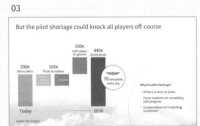

But the pilot shortage could knock all players off-course

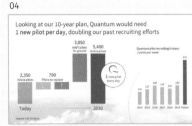

Looking at our 10-year plan, Quantum would need 1 new pilot per day, doubling our past recruiting efforts

To secure our **future**, we need to secure our share of **pilots**

⌐ Conflict ⌐   ⌐ BIG Idea ⌐

Marco continues with the WHAT

Our plan for winning critical new talent

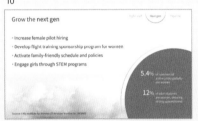

Grow the next gen

Our plan for winning critical new talent

⌐ Resolution ⌐

Transitional landing page is shown to handoff between speakers

Laura drills down into the second resolution bucket

Transitional landing page is shown to handoff between speakers

CASE STUDY

A team-piloted mission... for pilots

To see how an actual team story is built and delivered, let's revisit our Quantum Airlines story from *Chapter 10: Making a Recommendation.* The team at Quantum—Marco, Laura, Charlie, and Michelle—must build a deck to address the impending pilot shortage that could seriously impede the growth of the airline.

Here's a closer look at the role of each team member in the delivery of the Quantum story. Marco Vasquez, VP of People, is the emcee of the session. He kicks things off by introducing the setting (the growing airline industry), characters (passengers, airlines), and the conflict (the airline's inability to meet passenger demand due to a pilot shortage.)

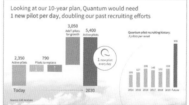

Speaker #1 delivers the WHY (setting, characters, conflict)

Then Marco hits the audience with the BIG Idea.

MARCO

Speaker #1 continues with the WHAT (BIG Idea)

From there, he previews the team's resolution for HOW they are going to resolve the pilot shortage and meet the skyrocketing global demand for more flights. Marco puts up the team's landing page, a clear visual cue that points to three paths the team is proposing to resolve the pilot shortage crisis and obtain new talent. He reviews the three buckets, which in preview are all shown in full color.

Speaker #1 previews the HOW (resolution) with a landing page

Then, with a simple transitional slide, Marco passes the baton to Charlie Wu, Director of Pilot Acquisition.

Transitional landing page to handoff between speakers

As Charlie hands things off, he flashes a transitional landing page which shows the resolution path that's on deck first. This path is made crystal clear by the "highlight and subdue" visual trick which smoothly signals—with content—where the next speaker will begin.

It's worth emphasizing that—*no matter what*—you don't want to lose story momentum when you move from speaker to speaker. As part of the build, these transitions should be encoded into the story with a brief, 30 second flash of the transitional landing page, to avoid awkward fumbling between speakers. Yes, this bulks up the deck, but a few extra slides are worth it for the guardrails it provides to the story.

And to take it a step further, it's a great idea to *pre-script* verbal transitions between speakers to help engineer a super-smooth hand-off and ensure meaty, content-driven transitions. But be aware that nothing you say should disrupt the flow of the story.

SPEAKER TRANSITIONS SHOULD ALWAYS BE DRIVEN BY THE CONTENT, NOT BY WHO'S SPEAKING NEXT.

So, instead of Marco transitioning through the speaker and saying what people commonly say (*"Charlie will continue with the next section"*), Marco will transition through content by showing the landing page and setting up the entire resolution of the story: *"We're going to discuss three paths to combat the pilot shortage: finding the right candidates, focusing on hiring female pilots, and widening our talent pipeline through partnership."* [He switches to the transitional landing page.] *"Charlie, our Director of Pilot Acquisition, will begin by showing how we're going to find the right candidates."*

At this point, Charlie takes over as the owner of the first resolution bucket and drills into enhanced pilot training, assessment, and screening.

CHARLIE

> 08
>
> ### Find the **right stuff**
>
> Right stuff   Next gen   Pipeline
>
> - Develop mentorship program to ensure flight-readiness
> - Implement new competency gap and pilot assessment
> - Launch adaptive, data-driven, customized training
> - Implement new screening and selection process
>
> **50%** of pilots flying by 2030 have not yet started to train
>
> **180K** pilots must transition to captains in next decade
>
> Source: CAE Airline Pilot Demand Outlook: 10-year View

Speaker #2 drills down into the first resolution "bucket"

When Charlie is finished, he then flashes the transitional landing page again. This time, however, the highlight is on the second bucket—Next gen focus—teeing up talent diversity expert Laura Singer to discuss hiring more female pilots. Again, this transition is driven by the content, not a lot of verbal preamble to the next speaker.

CHARLIE

LAURA

Transitional landing page to handoff between speakers

LAURA

Speaker #3 drills down into the second resolution "bucket"

And finally, Laura passes it along to Michelle DeAngelo, Director of Training and Development—again, by flashing the transitional landing page—teeing up the topic of how to increase the pipeline for new pilots.

LAURA

MICHELLE

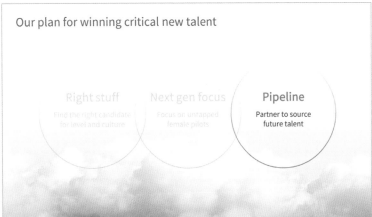

Transitional landing page to handoff between speakers

MICHELLE

Speaker #4 drills down into the third resolution "bucket"

After Michelle completes her section, she once again flashes the fully highlighted landing page to recap the three paths the team laid out. Repeating this slide provides both a great review of the resolution along with a visual handoff back to Marco to close out the story.

Review of resolution and final handoff between speaker #4 and #1

Speaker #1 revisits BIG Idea

Marco's close is to revisit the BIG Idea in more of a soundbite version. This is a great way to restate the purpose of the presentation in a slightly catchier way. (It feels less repetitive than using exactly the same words as before.) However, only use a soundbite if it feels natural. Don't force anything. You never want to introduce confusion at the very end of your story.

Have a plan, set the stage

At some point, everyone will work on a team that must coordinate and deliver ideas to move important business forward. So as you collaborate and approach your next big meeting or presentation, always have a plan and a process to guide both the build of your story and the choreography of your delivery. And remember, this is not only possible for teams of any size, it's critical.

It is important to note: the choreography shown in this Quantum Airlines story doesn't have to be tied to a visual story. In a less formal setting, the handoff from one teammate to another can just as easily be communicated verbally. However, we know that people are both auditory and visual learners. So for team stories, visuals will help you guide your audience and better retain your ideas.

CHAPTER 19

When Your Audience Is Virtual

YOU FINALLY SCORED that critical meeting with a room full of decision-makers. The only catch? The "room" is virtual. The slide deck you normally use for in-person meetings is rock-solid and well-tested. And like the busy, talented businessperson you are, you want to save time. You wonder: *Can't I just deliver the same story virtually?*

No, you can't.

Storytelling in an online environment is different. That same presentation (or training) deck you've used countless times in a conference room will play very differently in a virtual meeting.

What's so different?

VIRTUAL MEETINGS ARE A CHOREOGRAPHED DANCE BETWEEN YOUR STORY, YOUR VISUALS, AND YOUR PRESENCE.

To be able to pull off the virtual meeting "dance" you need three important ingredients:

1

Get your story straight

Yes, story. You've got to know your story backward and forwards for *any* meeting, but when everyone's behind a screen, you can't take any chances. A well-prepared narrative that uses your basic storytelling structure is a must.

2

Build in prescribed interaction

Why is pre-planned, built-in interaction necessary? Because the virtual world leaves *gaping* holes where natural body language or normal conversation would be. You must *engineer* a "natural" connection with your audience.

3

Let your virtual presence soar

Showing up with a well-prepared story, including visual and verbal cues to guide interaction, will make you appear nimble and responsive. Inside, you'll feel relaxed, in control, and confident, which ultimately will let your virtual presence soar.

How to inject prescribed interaction into any story

You can build frequent opportunities for interaction directly into your story using **interactive placeholder slides.** What are interactive placeholders? At the core, they're presentation slides that "direct virtual traffic." They *visually* show your audience what they need to know or do at any given moment. These *visual pauses* might signal a break for Q&A, a quick poll to check the audience's understanding, a discussion in chat, a virtual whiteboard brainstorming session, or even breakout rooms for small group exercises. Rather than you giving a constant monologue, interactive placeholder slides *guarantee* valuable feedback opportunities that will help you discover and directly address your audience's needs. *They are a lifeline for virtual meetings.*

STRONG VISUAL CUES

DIRECT YOUR VIRTUAL
AUDIENCE SO THEY KNOW
WHAT'S EXPECTED AND
HOW TO INTERACT

Here are some examples of interactive placeholder slides:

Now you might be wondering: *How do my interactive placeholder slides (which are part of my deck) co-exist with the actual tools available to me online like polls, whiteboard, chat, and more?* In short, interactive placeholders help bring online tools to life in a more dynamic, visual way. Here's how they work together:

Poll placeholder slide

 +

Poll

= Highly interactive virtual experience

Your presentation content *plus* your interactive visual placeholders are all contained in one file (that you either share or upload into a virtual meeting platform). Your interactive placeholders provide a visual cue for both you and your audience to signal when you'll be pausing for interaction and launching a specific tool. For example, if you want to check in with your audience using a poll, you'd first show your interactive placeholder slide and soon after, click to launch the poll (that ideally you've set up ahead of time). This combination of visual placeholders and tools leads to a well-guided, highly interactive virtual experience.

A word of caution

Virtual meeting platforms offer all kinds of fantastic interactive features and tools. But tools are never one size fits all. They should be used *intentionally,* not just because they're available. Your goal should always be to create meaningful, two-way dialogue between you and your virtual audience.

For example, a poll or breakout room is not appropriate for meetings with only a few participants. Instead, small groups would benefit from more intimate interactions like a discussion in chat or a brainstorming session via whiteboard annotations. Conversely, if your audience is large, then launching a poll, pausing for formal threaded Q&A, or using virtual breakout rooms can be a great option. Again, it's about using the right tool *mindfully,* based on audience size.

Here's a quick reference for using some common virtual tools across a variety of audiences:

	Small (1–10)	Medium (11–50)	Large (50+)
Breakout Sessions	✗	✔	✗
Chat	✔	✔	✗
Feedback Tools	✗	✔	✔
Polls	✗	✔	✔
Q&A	✗	✔	✔
Whiteboard	✔	✔	✗

Planned virtual interactions = more content than face-to-face

Ideally, plan for interactivity every three to five minutes or less, because your virtual audience will tune out if you go any longer than that. Yes, this means you will have more slides for virtual meetings than you're probably used to when delivering face-to-face presentations.

Virtual: 1 slide (or annotation) every 20 to 30 seconds

Face-to-face: 1 slide every 2 to 3 minutes

If you're still unsure about how to plan your virtual interaction, consider three questions: *How often do I want to check in? What type of information am I looking for? What kind of feedback will help me best navigate my story online?* Remember, everything comes down to anticipating the needs of your audience and getting the desired outcome of the meeting.

CASE STUDY

Planned interaction *in action*

Let's look at interactive placeholders in the context of a real business story. The following is a presentation delivered by Dr. Els van der Helm, a world-renowned sleep expert and CEO of Shleep. Shleep's corporate programs help organizations "invest" in their employee's well-being through sleep, resulting in a boost to the overall performance of the organization.[1] This story is the pitch Dr. van der Helm delivers to HR executives at all kinds of organizations.

01
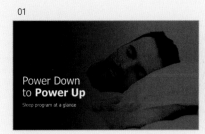

02

03

╰Setting & Characters╌╌╌

↑
Interaction

07

08

09

╰╌╌╌ *Conflict* ╌╌╌╯

↑
Interaction

13
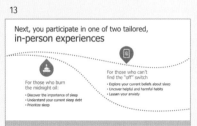

14

15

╌╌╌ *Resolution* ╌╌╌╯

↑
Interaction

04

05

06

Setting & Characters

Interaction

10

11

12

BIG Idea

Resolution

16

17

BIG Idea

Interaction

Notice how interaction is spliced into the narrative. It *begins* with an open discussion: it could be an opportunity to establish the desired outcomes for the meeting or in this case, a way to warm up a topic. Dr. van der Helm asks her audience to reflect and share about their own current sleep habits. She then introduces setting and characters to establish the context of the story: during our workday we [the characters] are always "on," slaves to our devices, powering through deadlines, [the work setting] striving to be amazing. But at night, we have trouble finding the "off" switch. She brings in supporting data: 20% of Americans get less than six hours of sleep. This context should paint a familiar picture of what's happening in the audience's world. But (and this is important), Dr. van der Helm never *assumes* her audience relates to her characters and setting. Instead, she takes another visual pause, asking: *What are the consequences when we don't get enough sleep?*

Conflict is now introduced, to show what's at risk if they *don't* take action. Her data shows that lack of sleep kills our behavioral skills, creativity, and overall health. Then once again, she pauses to engage her audience by introducing a poll that gauges how well the conflict is resonating with her audience. Next, she rolls out her BIG Idea (keep in mind, the one key message she wants her audience to remember): *We need rest and renewal to sustain high performance.* Finally, Dr. van der Helm rolls out her resolution, showcasing how her sleep program addresses poor sleep habits. She ends with a final visual placeholder slide to cue up a Q&A discussion about her solution.

So, what's the bottom line? Virtual meetings are *different* than face-to-face meetings. You can't just log on, scroll through your slides, and expect interaction to magically occur. You must carefully choreograph interaction by infusing it into a well-structured story—including a WHY, a WHAT, and a HOW—from beginning to end. Try this and you'll find that instead of being awkward or boring, virtual meetings can actually be very productive.

Let your virtual presence soar

So you're armed with a rock-solid story built with plenty of pre-planned interaction designed expressly for a virtual environment. But there's a human element that can't be ignored. The final piece is presence to pull it altogether. What is presence exactly? It's your ability to "read the virtual room" and fill in the gaps to avoid awkward silence or random chitchat that plague so many online meetings.

For example, use your preplanned visual pauses to interact with your audience but be sure to stay alert to long silences or delayed responses. If you sense you've lost focus or alignment, *check in.* It's always better to slow down your narrative and jump in with some impromptu interaction than lose people altogether.

Another way to boost your virtual presence is to *verbally* reinforce what your interactive placeholder slides are communicating *visually* onscreen. Why? Because you can expect some awkward silence when launching a poll, or pausing for Q&A, or the like. Your audience needs a moment to think and process what you just asked them to do. Therefore, be ready with some prescribed things to say to fill the void. Here are some examples to get you started.

What to say during a poll

> I want to hear from you. Let's go ahead and open up with a short poll...

> Do you agree or disagree? Please take a moment to vote in our poll. Remember to click the submit button.

> Let's take a quick moment to get your feedback... I'm going to open a poll...

What to say when asking for feedback

> If you want to ask a question, raise your hand and unmute your line. I'd love to hear from you.

> If you can hear my voice, please raise your hand.

> Have you ever [question]? If yes, click the green check mark. If no, click the red X.

What to say when launching a chat discussion

Turn your direction to the chat panel. We've just posted some important links for you to reference after today's session.

If you have a comment, please simply type directly in the chat panel and send to everyone.

Please take a moment to give me your feedback in chat. I want to hear from you!

IN SHORT...

Virtual meetings are here to stay

Everyone needs to be prepared to lead a successful virtual meeting. Although online meetings lack the kind of body language face-to-face meetings have, it's absolutely possible to engineer in *virtual* body language. If you come armed with a rock-solid story with plenty of pre-planned interaction, you're sure to run a smooth, controlled meeting *that is* responsive to your audience's needs from beginning to end. The result? The control and dexterity you gain will seriously boost your confidence and let your executive presence soar.

RECAP

Adapting Your Story for Different Audiences

YOU HAVE YOUR AUDIENCE MANIFESTO

To build a powerful story, always keep your audience in mind. First, start with a few foundational audience questions and considerations. We've also outlined some common scenarios that come up in business communications which would require you to make adjustments to your story. Once again, everything begins with your audience and your baseline story structure.

1

Audience first

Your audience should always be the first consideration in your story. Investigate their perspective and role wherever possible. This will affect the order and level of detail in your story.

2

The pivot strategy

Your most demanding audiences are time-crunched executives, trying to make a decision. One of your best strategies is to be prepared to tell your story nonlinearly and *pivot* to address their needs and questions in the moment.

3

Diverse audiences

One-size audience does not fit all. Be prepared to grow your story to directly address an audience with variable needs.

There are many other reasons that you might need to expand, contract, or diversify your story structure. These are just some of the most common ones. If you stick with your baseline story structure, you will always have the control you need to make the most of every business conversation.

Audience. Structure. A Flexible Story.

Got it? Let's move on.

4

No more than three to five slides

As a way to control overlong meetings, people are often restricted to just a few slides. Don't worry—you can truncate your story signposts and still have plenty of time to walk through a meaningful resolution.

5

Team storytelling

Team stories should be built on a common framework and delivered like a choreographed dance. Decide together the WHY, WHAT, and a *preview* of the story's HOW in order to then split up, and work on individual parts of the HOW.

6

Virtual audiences

Virtual audiences are different and you must adjust your story accordingly. Have a well-developed narrative, filled with preplanned interaction, using both verbal and visual cues. The result? You'll become a more nimble, responsive, and confident storyteller.

PART 6

All together now: Building a Common Language of Storytelling

CHAPTER 20

Fostering a Culture of Story Coaches

WELL DONE. You've made it through the basics of business storytelling. You discovered the building blocks of a great story, understand the critical role of a BIG Idea, and have learned to craft active headlines. You've seen dozens of examples of the whole thing in action. We hope you're inspired.

But to make sure you (and your colleagues) grab for these tools and this system every time you want to sell your ideas, they must be embedded into your day-to-day process. Even more, they need to be part of your organizational culture.

BUSINESS STORYTELLING HAS THE GREATEST EFFECT WHEN IT'S INSTILLED IN THE CULTURE OF AN ORGANIZATION.

We've all witnessed business trends that have swept into town and then left just as quickly (Blackberry, we hardly knew ya). Storytelling is not one of them. Remember, we've been telling stories for thousands of years—just not usually to advance business. So how can you go from "hey, storytelling sounds like something we should do" to actually making it an everyday team practice?

It starts with building and reinforcing a culture of storytelling that will permeate your team, department and, eventually your organization. Amazingly, it's not that complicated. In fact, getting everyone to speak "story" in your organization requires one main change in your everyday process:

Coaching.

That's right. You need to have a regular practice of both **manager** and **peer-to-peer coaching.** And it needs to be spearheaded by managers.

Coaching, top-down and side-to-side

These days, managers are expected to do more than issue directives or be arms-length advisors. Great managers are also great coaches. They support and mentor their staff and help them to grow in their role. And they also do something else: reinforce the practice of coaching *amongst their team.*

When managers encourage peer-to-peer coaching and a highly collaborative environment, it makes a remarkable difference. Josh Bersin, an industry analyst and founder of Bersin by Deloitte, studied the effects of coaching and found that systematic, manager-driven coaching develops significantly better leaders and boosts employee retention.[1]

So you might be thinking: *Great, but what does all this coaching have to do with storytelling?* A whole lot. When manager or peer-to-peer coaching is regularly integrated into the story building process, storytelling skills skyrocket. Being coached helps people see how well they edited their ideas, insights, and data, and weaved them into a strong narrative that follows a clear, logical path. What's more, coaches help their teammates determine if their story was well-targeted toward the intended audience.

THE MORE THAT PEER AND MANAGER COACHING IS KNITTED INTO OUR STORY DEVELOPMENT PROCESS, THE MORE IT WILL SEEP INTO THE LARGER CULTURE.

Bottom line, when coaching happens regularly, storytelling skills rapidly advance at all levels.

Story coaching starts with managers

To all managers who want to encourage rampant storytelling on their team, *great idea!* But a word of warning: pushing this change is largely in their hands. After all, it's the managers who are charged with locking in day-to-day team processes and storytelling is no different than any other process. If these leaders want it to become second nature to their staff, *they need to model it.*

MANAGERS MUST SIGNAL
TO STAFF THAT
IT'S SAFE TO SHARE IDEAS
EVEN IF, INITIALLY, THEY FAIL

But there are a couple of obstacles to this type of regular collaboration. The first one is time. We all seem to be in a race to deliver everything quickly. It seems faster to just shut our doors and build a story on our own. But hasty delivery of our ideas is always short-sighted. People that receive regular story coaching find that it actually *saves* them time since their (coached) story will always result in a stronger and more succinct final product. And this is true ongoing. Regular coaching makes people ever more adept at targeting and selling their ideas.

The second obstacle is that people often feel uncomfortable sharing ideas that might not be fully thought through. They're worried they'll get it wrong, look foolish, or seem amateurish. So, to truly foster a culture of great storytellers, managers must do everything they can to ease their team's insecurity about sharing.

When managers regularly coach their staff—and reassure them that it's okay to iterate and get it wrong—the team will begin to feel more comfortable coaching each other. And then an even greater benefit emerges... a common language.

Peer-to-peer story coaching gets teams speaking in "story"

Business stories are rarely prepared and delivered by one person in isolation. More often, people collaborate on a deck or strategy as part of a team mission. (For more on this, see *Chapter 18: Team Presentations: Who Does What?)* That mission is made infinitely easier when everyone uses a common story framework, a distinct vocabulary (like the four signposts, BIG Idea, active headlines), and generally shares a story mindset.

Coaching and being coached leads to storytelling fluency and better team storytelling.

A LOOK AHEAD

What exactly does coaching entail?

More than advising, coaching is actually *questioning*.

In the bestselling book *The Coaching Habit, Say Less, Ask More & Change the Way You Lead Forever*, Michael Bungay Stanier makes the crucial point that it's the central job of any coach to *ask the questions behind the narrative*.[2]

People aren't necessarily born to be great coaches. But it's not that hard to learn how to systematically question the logic and assumptions made in a story. Since story coaching begins with managers, let's start with them.

CHAPTER 21

Five Ways Managers Can Reinforce Storytelling

SO MANAGERS (or future managers), we're talking just to you now. You know that it's your move to drive the culture of storytelling by being a model coach yourself *and* encouraging your team to coach each other. *No small feat.* So, to make your role even clearer, let's boil things down to five valuable ways you can immediately jumpstart and reinforce a culture of both storytelling and story coaching.

1. Reinforce to your staff *who* their audience is

Even when a similar story is presented over and over again—like a product pitch—audiences can shift dramatically. People might come from varying industries, serve different roles, and operate at different levels. One of the ways managers can best coach storytellers is to remind them to *carefully* consider who they will face and make sure they've shifted their narrative to best suit that specific audience.

2. Remind your team: storytelling opportunities are everywhere

Once a team has learned classic storytelling structure and how it applies to business stories, the opportunities to use it are infinite. Particularly when team members are fairly new to business storytelling, managers should encourage them to find ways to use the framework in all types of communications. This can include emails, marketing collateral, phone conversations, or elevator pitches.

Every time managers point out these opportunities, it helps to enrich awareness and build on the storytelling culture.

3. Encourage ongoing peer-to-peer coaching

Managers should do everything they can to model and integrate peer-to-peer coaching into the story building process. The best way to get started? Make it official. Assign peer-coaching partnerships or let the team self-select partners.

To really reinforce this practice, have teams share the results of coaching sessions during staff meetings. Have them discuss:

> ✓ *What path did your coaching questions take?*

> ✓ *How did the coaching session change the story from beginning to end?*

> ✓ *What was the ultimate outcome of the story?*

This is the most visible way for everyone to see the value of peer-to-peer coaching. (More on this in *Chapter 22: Ready, Set, Coach! Five Tips for Peer-to-Peer Story Coaching.*)

4. Set high expectations... with the promise of real career advancement

Managers should make sure this message is clear: while practicing storytelling is a great skill-building exercise, the ultimate goal is to *measurably* improve business outcomes. Make sure you set high expectations for your team's work and challenge them to tell stories with clear, tangible results. Stories should always be built to deliver on a goal.

5. Consider formal storytelling training

Managers who are really serious about encouraging a culture of widespread storytelling should bring in formal training. Training is an effective way to bring the team together to learn strategies, ask questions, receive peer-to-peer and professional coaching, and get equipped to immediately apply their learnings on the job. Best yet, good trainers will always provide heavy reinforcement tools to help people use their training long past the day of learning.

IN SHORT...

Stories will advance company and professional goals

If you need one more way to encourage storytelling on your team, here's a bonus:

Remind staff that not only will these skills help the team and the company achieve their goals, they will also help them as individuals grow in their roles and advance their careers. For managers, there's simply nothing more gratifying to coach an individual, see them master their storytelling skills, and learn to confidently "own the room."

Managers can have a huge impact on the development of their team's storytelling skills, but you know who'll ultimately have a much bigger impact? The team themselves. *On each other.*

IT'S A TEAM'S EVERYDAY
COACHING OF ONE ANOTHER
THAT WILL MAKE
STORYTELLING SKILLS SOAR

CHAPTER 22

Ready, set, coach!

Five Tips for Peer-to-Peer Story Coaching

SO WE KNOW THAT STORYTELLING is driven by coaching, and coaching starts with managers. But managers cannot coach their whole team all of the time. The bedrock of storytelling culture is peer-to-peer coaching.

Peer coaching encourages storytelling in an organization in three important ways. First, it gives individual contributors an *available* sounding board to try out ideas. Too often, we work in isolation and don't ask for feedback from others or we're reluctant to disturb our busy managers. In a peer coaching friendly environment, people shed their fear of "stealing" someone's time because having a teammate review your story draft is simply part of the story development process.

Second, teammates can really help keep each other on message. They'll be able to quickly help identify where added facts, data, and ideas are helping to *strengthen* the story and where oversharing information is detracting from the main points.

And finally, peer coaches will help determine how well facts, data, and ideas map to a story structure. This inquiry should include the four signposts, a BIG Idea, active headlines, and anything else that might strengthen the story.

Here are five fundamental coaching questions peers should ask

As we said in *Chapter 20: Fostering a Culture of Story Coaches*, peer-to-peer coaching must be modeled and encouraged by managers. The good news is that anyone can coach a teammate with some pointed questions that'll help keep them accountable to their ideas.

1. Does the story *definitively* address each of the four signposts?

Here's where having an *uber-simple* storytelling framework really helps. Use it as a roadmap to make it very easy to "check the box" on how well your peer's story maps to the classic story structure.

For starters, examine if the story actually establishes a true **setting:**

Setting

✓ *Does it reveal concrete knowledge of the audience's world?*

✓ *Does it spell out the dynamic in a market or company they care about?*

Make sure it includes well-defined **characters:**

Characters

✓ *Does it have meaningful characters that clearly represent the audience?*

✓ *Are characters contending with issues their audience actually cares about?*

Check that the story builds to a real **conflict:**

✓ *Does the conflict demonstrate understanding of the audience's problems?*

✓ *Does it spell out consequences for the characters (i.e. the audience)?*

✓ *Does the conflict spring from obvious tension language using words and phrases such as "However," "But," or "To make matters worse…"*

Conflict

And finally, ensure the story's **resolution** actually addresses the conflict:

Resolution

✓ *Is the story's resolution satisfying?*

✓ *Does it go into enough detail… or too much detail?*

✓ *Does the story prove that the resolution, when enacted, will achieve the glorious benefits of the BIG Idea?*

And speaking of the BIG Idea…

2. Is there a concise, memorable BIG Idea?

As a coach, helping your peer get their **BIG Idea** *spot on* is perhaps the most important service you can provide. A solid BIG Idea is the lynchpin of the story framework and one of the earliest story elements to construct. Here's how to help them "gut check" it. Examine:

BIG Idea

✓ How well did your peer state what their BIG Idea is, and its specific benefit(s)?

✓ Does every other fact, piece of data, or idea included in the story directly support the BIG Idea?

✓ Is there an obvious way to turn a longer BIG Idea into a conversational soundbite?

Tip for teams: When a team is developing a story together, it's a best to agree on the BIG Idea early, before anyone is tempted to pull in slides from old decks or pile on data that might be relevant. Alignment on the BIG Idea helps avert the disastrous *Frankendeck* we discussed in *Chapter 9: Five Well-Tested Ways to Visualize Your Story.*

3. Does the resolution support the BIG Idea?

The **resolution** is the concluding part of your peer's story. It's easy for a story to get derailed as the narrative dives into the nitty-gritty details. The resolution—perhaps features of a product, the timeline of an initiative, or interim milestones of a proposed software integration—is critical to edit properly in order not to bog down the story. Make sure your peer is not taking the wind out of their own story sails by helping them moderate the *amount* of information they offer in the resolution. Ask them:

✓ Is there enough detail here so that your audience can reasonably make a decision?

Resolution

✓ Do they have more details ready in case the audience asks for more?

✓ Does every detail included in the resolution push the BIG Idea forward?

THE BIGGEST FUNCTION YOU PROVIDE AS A COACH IS EDITOR.

Advise your teammate: *less detail is often more (but always have more ready).*

Help them cut secondary details that will weigh down their narrative. But as you coach them—and act as their proxy audience—question them further to make sure they are prepared to handle an aggressively inquisitive executive or key stakeholder. They may need to be prepared with hidden slides or perhaps a handout to offer anyone who wants to go deeper into the weeds.

4. Do the story headlines flow?

Coaches, it's reading time. As you go over the story, determine how well your peer used their headlines from the beginning to the end of the narrative. Ask:

Headlines

✓ *Does every new headline build on the one before?*

✓ *Does every headline serve as a transition statement that moves the story forward?*

✓ *Do headlines flow and sound conversational?*

As we mentioned in *Chapter 7: Push Your Story Forward with Active Headlines,* one of the best exercises to test how well headlines are written, is to simply read them out loud. And again, they should make narrative sense just on their own.

5. What else can improve the story?

This final peer coaching challenge might seem kind of extraneous. Your teammate has their story structure nailed, their BIG Idea looming large over everything else, and active story headlines that keep it all chugging along... so, what else could there be to do? *A lot.*

It's your role as peer coach to help guide that extra push that'll mean the difference between a good story and GREAT one. Ask your teammate to think:

From good to great

✓ *Are there any ideas, data, or insights that could use more emphasis in order to take the audience on a more memorable journey?*

✓ *Is there any part of the story that goes on too long? Did your peer belabor any point that, when cut, would make for a sharper story?*

✓ *Is there any place where your peer is struggling to explain? If so, now is the time to make sure they have their story down pat.*

It never fails, no matter how solid a story seems, there is always a way to take it to the next level. And in our hurry-up world, this final step is usually skipped. Our advice? Slow down. Observe the story holistically and help your peer identify where a few final tweaks will make their story go from good to great.

IN SHORT...

Peer-to-peer coaching makes a storytelling culture flourish. Teammates keep each other on message, and help people recognize how well their chosen facts and data promote that message. Checking one another for the four signposts, a solid BIG Idea—supported by the resolution—and active story headlines truly improves story quality for entire teams.

RECAP

Coaching Drives Storytelling

Widespread storytelling springs from a culture of coaching that must be modeled by leaders, practiced between peers, and become one of the team's everyday processes. Everything hinges on a common understanding of the storytelling framework.

1

The coaching process

Managers must drive *and* reinforce a culture of coaching by doing it directly and encouraging their team to share and question each other's stories. Coaching should be a regular part of the story development process.

2

Tips for managers

Managers can immediately support storytelling in five ways: helping establish a clear target audience, pointing out diverse storytelling opportunities, encouraging peer-to-peer coaching, setting clear (and high) standards, and bringing in formal storytelling training. Managers should tie great storytelling to career advancement.

3

Tips for peers

Peer-to-peer coaching requires people to ask questions in a safe environment. They should help each other stay on message, and ensure strict adherence to the story framework—including the four signposts, BIG Idea, and active headlines that flow—to help build clear and succinct stories.

A Final Word From the Sisters

AND SO YOU'VE MADE IT. You're at the end of this book but at the beginning of a storytelling journey that will help propel your ideas—and your career—forward. To send you off, let's get a quick reminder of what you're taking with you:

- **You're armed with a simple, repeatable, story-driven framework**—along with power tools such as active headlines and essential visual techniques—to organize and prioritize your ideas.

- **You know how to flex your narrative to fit changing scenarios** such as time cut short, an audience with diverse needs, or having to adapt your story for a virtual environment.

- **You have a clear path to career advancement** because you now know how to easily and consistently apply a story arc to your *everyday* communications. You have better control over how decision-makers hear your ideas and, more and more, outcomes will be engineered by *you*.

Not only will this book be your essential guide for how to build business stories, it will also be a resource for dozens of real business scenarios—visual presentations, emails, one-pagers, and more—that show this storytelling framework in action.

GROUNDED IN THEORY BUT SMOTHERED IN PRACTICALITY, THIS IS A FRAMEWORK YOU CAN USE EVERY DAY.

We *know* how high the stakes are to get your ideas heard over the noise, resistance, and so often, big egos. We've taught thousands of talented, smart people for over 20 years. If you *cringed* when you recognized your last presentation or email in our "before" examples, rest assured—you're not alone. In our workshops, we observe (often emotional) reactions to our before and after story makeovers. Teams from world-class, Fortune 500 companies tell us over and over again: *"I have literally made every mistake you pointed out,"* or *"I don't know whether to laugh or cry,"* or (wistfully) *"No one has ever shown me any other way."*

We get it. Everyone needs to move fast and perform. Many of us simply default to what we can get our hands on, leveraging content for a "quick fix." We grab old slides, borrow charts from a co-worker, or perhaps swipe something pretty from the marketing team. And we wind up with the narrative mess we've dubbed the *Frankendeck*—slides jammed with bullet points, impossible-to-read data, and scrambled messages. The audience has no idea what we want them to know and do. There's no clear call to action. The conversation stops cold. *Frankendecks* amount to an incalculable loss of opportunity.

Can we all agree? #nomorefrankendecks

And yet despite the decks, emails, and proposals flying around, riddled with confusing messages, companies rarely teach a better way. And that is why, dear product manager (or salesperson or data engineer), we wrote this book. No more muddled messages. No more firehosing data. No more missed opportunities.

Here's our challenge to you: use this framework to approach all your business communications with intention, mindfulness and a strategy. "Exercise" it and, like any other workout you practice, you'll become a better, stronger storyteller. Pretty soon, you'll be recognizing opportunities everywhere, every day to structure your ideas into the arc of a story.

No one's ever shown you another way? You've now been shown. Your everyday business storytelling journey starts right now.

Onward!

Janine Lee

Gratitude

Special thanks to all the amazing humans in our life who helped make *Everyday Business Storytelling* a reality.

Julia Pickar: Our written voice (just better)
Becky Nelson: Art direction and illustration
Julie Terberg: Visual design
Daren Lewis and Hisako Esaki: Story development
Kitta Bodmer: Author photography

To our TPC "work family" who played a critical role in bringing the vision of this book to life:
Lauren Kuykendall: Marketing maven
Carlie Johnston: Project manager extraordinaire

And to the rest of our TPC family who didn't directly play a role in this book but who "kept the lights on" so we could make it happen: **Bob Seiler, Simon Gottheiner, Katie Matthews, Kevin Campbell, Meghan Costella and Shelby Milne.**

To our mentors and champions

Tom Floyd, for always believing in us, getting us out of "PowerPoint jail" and inviting "Frankendeck" and "hot mess" into our daily vocabulary.
Michael Streefland, for giving us the courage to say "no."
Nicki Bouton, for guiding us in the early days.
Michael Bigelow, for being one of our earliest fans.
Lauren Goldstein, for being our "unofficial" advisor and queen of networking.
Randa Brooks, for being a mentor and guiding force on the financial growth of our business.
Ian Gates, for always helping us protect what's rightfully ours.

To our parents

Thank you for showing us how to "show up" in life and in work and for giving us the gift of sisterhood.

To our children

Jacob, Zoe, Ava, Hadley and Liam, you are our North Stars. THANK YOU for inspiring us every day to work our hardest and giving us the greatest thing in life to "show up" for... you.

To our hubbies

Howard and Simon, thank you for putting up with our *meshugas* since the beginning. You have been our sounding boards, our sanity checkers, and our greatest cheerleaders as we've navigated growing a business and our families.

To my big sister

Lee, you are my GPS roadmap. I would be lost without you—in life and in business. – *Janine*

To my little sister

Janine, this book begins and ends with you. Your vision, passion and creativity has led us to this moment, and I could not imagine my work or personal life without you at the center of it. – *Lee*

About the Authors

Janine Kurnoff and Lee Lazarus are Silicon Valley–bred sisters (now based in Portland, OR) who have helped hundreds of teams at top brands worldwide become strategic, visual communicators. Janine and Lee co-founded The Presentation Company (TPC) in 2001 and have never looked back.

Janine is the passionate, visionary chief architect behind TPC's award-winning workshops. Lee is the marketing and sales maven who "gets" the customer mindset and will be first to spot a trend. The result? A powerhouse team that constantly innovates and strives for excellence.

Our backstory

Prior to founding The Presentation Company, Janine worked for Yahoo! Inc. in sales training and later as an on-air webcast host where she interviewed some of Silicon Valley's top CEOs, market strategists, and Hollywood celebrities. Janine received her MBA in International Business from the Monterey Institute of International Studies. She is an accomplished keynote speaker and contributes her expertise to publications such as *Forbes, Training Industry*, and *Inc.* magazines. Lee spent a decade developing the branding, marketing communications, and PR strategy for two of the fastest-growing Internet and telecommunications market research firms in Silicon Valley. Lee received her BA from Boston University's renowned College of Communication.

In their spare time

Janine can be found most days in a barre class, chasing her three high-energy children, or enjoying a much-needed date night with her husband. Lee is equally obsessed with a great workout (hello burpees!), cooking with her two teenagers, snuggling her Cavapoo, and long, scenic drives with her husband.

Notes & Photo Credits

The following fictitious companies that appear in this book are examples of real business stories developed exclusively by The Presentation Company LLC: *GO Insurance, Bastion Mobile, Nirvana Tech, Harmony Health, Quantum Airlines, LearnForward.*

Due to confidentiality, all company names, company background information, company data, and industry facts are fictitious and used solely for learning purposes.

PART 1

Chapter 1
1. Sperry, Roger, "Left-Brain, Right-Brain," *Saturday Review* (Aug. 9, 1975): pp. 30–33.

Chapter 2
1. Klein, Gary, *Seeing What Others Don't: The Remarkable Ways We Gain Insights* (March 24, 2015): p. 22.

PART 4

Chapter 12
1. https://www.mckinsey.com/industries/technology-media-and-telecommunications/our-insights/the-social-economy#by and 2019 HBR article: https://hbr.org/2019/01/how-to-spend-way-less-time-on-email-every-day

PART 5

Chapter 19
1. Dr. Els van der Helm is a world-leading sleep expert and CEO of Shleep. Shleep focuses on improving the health of companies by improving the well-being of employees through a digital sleep coaching platform.

PART 6

Chapter 20
1. Bersin & Associates, "High-Impact Performance Management: Maximizing Performance Coaching," (Nov. 14, 2012).
2. Stanier, Michael Bungay, *The Coaching Habit: Say Less, Ask More & Change the Way You Lead Forever* (Feb. 29, 2016), p. 12.

PHOTO CREDITS

Index

Ready to up-level your storytelling skills?

Keep learning...

The Presentation Company's highly experiential, award-winning workshops will transform you or your team from data collectors into authentic visual storytellers.

What you'll get:

- Work on your own story and receive coaching to ensure real behavior change
- Receive valuable resources and toolkits to jumpstart your storytelling journey
- Get tips for creating compelling visuals that you won't find anywhere else

Don't have time?

We've got you covered. Whether you're looking for face-to-face, virtual, or digital on-demand training, we offer a variety of flexible delivery options to fit your busy schedule.

Let's Chat!   WWW.PRESENTATION-COMPANY.COM

THE PRESENTATION COMPANY™